Beowulf:
A Guide to Study

by
Marijane Osborn

Wipf & Stock
PUBLISHERS
Eugene, Oregon

Wipf and Stock Publishers
199 West 8th Avenue, Suite 3
Eugene, Oregon 97401

Beowulf
A Guide to Study
By Osborn, Marijane
Copyright©1986 by Osborn, Marijane
ISBN: 1-59244-727-9
Publication date 6/15/2004
Previously published by Pentangle Press, 1986

For Fred
who guided me *in geardagum*
swa he nu git deð

Some Major Correspondences
in *Beowulf*

Prologue
- A. Panegyric for Scyld
- B. Scyld's funeral
- C. History of Danes before Hrothgar
- D. Hrothgar's order to build Heorot

First fight
- Grendel's unexpected night attack
- Sea voyage to Denmark
- Greeting by hosts
  - Hrothgar
  - Unferth
  - Wealhtheow
- *Fight with Grendel* (see Diagram 3)

Interlude (Great banquet, nightfall)

Second fight
- Grendel's dam's unexpected night attack
- *Fight with Grendel's Dam* (see Diagram 4)

Interlude
- Banquet, nightfall
- Farewell to hosts
- Sea voyage home
- Reception in Geatland

Third fight
- Dragon's unexpected night attack
- *Fight with Dragon* (see Diagram 5)

Epilogue
- D. Beowulf's order to build his barrow
- C. History of Geats after Beowulf ("messenger's prophecy")
- B. Beowulf's funeral
- A. Eulogy for Beowulf.

Rene Derolez (on studying *Beowulf*):
My fellow students and I had the impression of entering a vast new territory, but one that had been often and thoroughly explored. . . . But the maps with which all these explorers had provided us were not entirely satisfactory.

Susan Sontag:
To understand something is to understand its topography, to know how to chart it. And to know how to get lost.

The diagram opposite is taken with the permission of John D. Niles from his article "Ring Composition and the Structure of *Beowulf*," *PMLA* 94 (1979); the other diagrams referred to in this one will be found in that article.

Table of Contents

Introduction

The purpose of this guide is to answer a few of the major questions about *Beowulf* for those who want no more than that, and to map the way into a complex area of scholarship for those who wish to go farther. Though it may be used with any edition or translation of the poem, the guide has been designed to supplement my own translation of *Beowulf,* and that is the text I have used throughout.

Sometime during the Anglo-Saxon period, perhaps in the ninth century, a Christian poet composed *Beowulf,* drawing on earlier Scandinavian traditions. The only surviving manuscript is a late tenth-century copy.* Though external evidence shows that the poet knew certain traditions of Swedish history and made use of a number of tales that were well-circulated in the North (such as that of the hero's battle with the walking dead), there are no direct references in other works of the period to the hero Beowulf or to the poem about him. Ever since the poem was first edited and published in 1815, the lack of contemporary

*Although the traditional opinion is that the *Beowulf* manuscript was transcribed in the West Saxon dialect some two centuries after its composition, Kevin S. Kiernan has recently made the revolutionary assertion that one of the two scribes copying the poem may have been the poet himself, who made revisions in the manuscript we have: *Beowulf and the Beowulf Manuscript* (New Brunswick, N.J.: Rutgers University Press, 1981). Other scholars are also arguing for a later (post-Viking) date on the basis of reassessments of historical, linguistic and archaeological data.

references, the hints of Christianity and symbolism in the work, and its puzzling structure have resulted in fierce arguments about when and where *Beowulf* was actually composed, for what audience it was intended, what it means, why various elements are combined as they are, and how conscious an artist the poet was. Though philologists have studied the poem for over a century and a half, and clearer meanings continue to emerge even today, it is still not always certain what is meant by the words in the text. As recently as Klaeber's edition, the style and structure of *Beowulf* were still being judged by classical or modern standards having little to do with the poem, and thus often attacked for the very qualities now recognized as virtues. In this guide I have sketched out some of these problems and the scholarly and critical solutions to them that have been developed over the years.

Klaeber's great edition is likely to be the text used by someone going on to read *Beowulf* in the original. While I have omitted his categories that are not relevant to a translation, otherwise I have modelled this discussion on his overall format: fabulous elements, history, the Christian "coloring," structure, and style. (A sampling of textual problems is discussed in the notes to my translation.) I have tried to bring the discussions up to date without going too deeply into any single subject, with the exception of the ambivalent Christianity in the poem: how Christian a poem is it? The emphasis placed by scholars on this aspect of *Beowulf*, my own strong views on the subject, and even the nature of my translation have prompted me to a comparatively extended discussion in this case.

Marijane Osborn
University of California
at Davis

I   The Main Plot: Beowulf and the Monsters

In the midst of a huge, shadowy and primeval world, a Danish king named Hrothgar decides to build a great hall which men will hear of forever. It will be roofed with gold, and in it Hrothgar will give good things to others as freely as God has been generous to him. The new hall, Heorot, is duly built and Hrothgar's people are happy there as in a newly created Eden, when suddenly a "grim guest" comes from the dark, aroused by the sound of the harp. His name is Grendel, and he comes in hatred of fellowship. No one can stop him from killing the king's chosen warriors and drinking their blood.

Motive

Grendel takes over Heorot and "rules" alone by night for twelve years. Far away, Beowulf, a young prince of the Swedish Geats, hears about the hall of friendship rendered useless by a monster, and he comes to fight Grendel, in unarmed combat because Grendel "does not know the use of weapons." Beowulf succeeds in cleansing Heorot of the monster; during the wrestling match, so violent that the great hall itself is threatened, Beowulf tears off Grendel's arm, and the monster flees howling into the misty moors to die.

1

The next day and evening the Danes are relaxed and happy—too soon, because Grendel has a mother. The rejoicing in Heorot is once more an innocent prelude to tragedy, and it is the king's best friend who is killed this time. Beowulf hears of this the next morning and sets out at once to fight the mother in her own lair, a damp, hall-like cavern entered through a dismal lake. This is a more difficult and uncertain fight. Beowulf attempts to use a sword, but it fails him; he does not know that the monsters cannot be touched by ordinary weapons. Grendel's mother nearly kills him; when her first dagger-blow is deflected by Beowulf's armor, she straddles him and strikes again. But the firelight leaps up and Beowulf glimpses a giant sword hanging on the wall. He twists away, snatches the sword, and manages to behead the water-witch, striking through her neck bone. When exploring the depths of the underwater lair, he finds Grendel lying dead, and beheads him also. This suggests that the monsters are trolls, which may only be slain finally by beheading. Beowulf takes Grendel's head and the golden sword-hilt as trophies to the king; the blade of the sword has been melted by the heat of the monsters' blood.

At the feast that night the king, Hrothgar, makes a speech, after gazing for a time upon the golden sword-hilt. Power, like strength or wealth, can make a man heedless, he says, so that he is open to the unexpected, both within and without. Take Heremod, once king of the Danes: he became great, but then turned miserly, and his death showed how futile that was! God is often generous to men, but this sometimes deceives them, first into complacency and then into unsatisfied desire (like Heremod's). Yet change always comes, whether as illness, disaster, or death. Take me, Hrothgar: I was also a great king, and made peace on all my borders and ruled well, then Grendel came. Thank God I see his head here now! (I interpret the moral of Hrothgar's sermon thus: if God is generous to you, then give, do not withhold. I believe that it is to be understood by those listening in Heorot within the context Hrothgar offers of inevitable change.)

Beowulf goes home richer in fame, treasures and good advice (which is, like gold, a gift of rulers, equally sought). But as he recounts his Danish adventures to his own lord, the king of the Geats, it seems that in retrospect the monsters have become more folkloristic and the political situation in Heorot more real.

Late in life Beowulf himself becomes a ruler. When he is old, as Hrothgar was, change comes unexpectedly. A thief awakens strife by stealing a golden cup from a treasure guarded by a sleeping dragon—dragons, of course, are the arch non-givers. When he misses the cup, the aroused dragon comes out from his barrow raging and burning indiscriminately. His wrath is not specific, like that of the Grendel-kind, but general, like that of a giant hornet whose nest has been disturbed. He burns the king's gift-hall, the seat of human generosity, and thereby endangers the value-structure of the kingdom; the gift-throne of a Germanic hall has nearly the value of an altar, and the gifts that are presented from the throne simultaneously bestow praise and confirm allegiance like a modern wedding ring or a medal of honor. Beowulf, whose special gift from God is the ability to slay the monsters who threaten the gift-throne, the center of human allegiance, must fight the dragon, old as he is, with the help of a young kinsman, Wiglaf. Beowulf kills the dragon, but the dragon also wounds him fatally.

Beowulf dies happy, thinking he has won the dragon's gold, and hence a new gift-hall, for his people. But his people promptly proceed, in their own generosity and love for Beowulf, to bury the dragon gold with him—"as useless to men as it was before," comments the poet. This loss of the gold so sacrificially won is the final ironic futility of the poem, but at the same time the treasure also is a great gift of love and honor in the face of fate, first from Beowulf to his people, then from the people to their dead king. Human solidarity wins even over devastating loss as Beowulf's people, faced now with exile, sing an elegy in his praise.

Some Further Analysis of the Poet's Design

This is the main design of the story, but there is much shading of detail. For example, within the frames of the lavish ship-burial of Shield Shefing, the founding king of Denmark, at the beginning of the poem, and Beowulf's own funeral pyre at the end, the poem moves from a sort of "dreamtime" toward real history. *Beowulf* has always been considered by Scandinavian historians as a mine of information and confirmation for things known from archaeology and hinted at in sagas. But this real history occurs, curiously, in the part of the poem dominated by the most mythical of the monsters, the dragon. As the surrounding events move from myth into history, the monsters move away from the human toward the symbolic, and even the locations of the fights may be said to follow this progression away from the human center: darkened hall, underwater hall, barrow (treasure grave). Each fight takes place further away from the life represented by Heorot in feast time.

Along with the Scandinavian myth-history in the Danish part of the poem, we, the audience, are given a glimmer of scriptural history which sheds light on the monster fights: they are part of the Great Feud dominating human history from Eden until the Apocalypse. But of course this level of the history of mankind is only between us and the poet; it is suppressed in the pagan world of the poem. The sixth century Scandinavians apprehend the monsters coming unexpected from the dark much more "existentially"!

The three monsters are associated with the void that stands in contrast to the lighted hall of friendship. The Grendels are like that ghostly creature known to some cultures even today, perhaps once human, now no longer quite human in shape, a giant haunter of waste places, having enormous glowing eyes which, if they catch you in their glare, will quite literally petrify you. You can't move unless it turns away—which, as it gains strength from the blood of those who dwell in tribal friendship, it is not likely to do! (Arctic Indian villages abound with tales of such monsters, which also may be found in Gypsy and Lappish lore, to name only those folk cultures with which I am most familiar.) The dragon is quite different both in its monstrousness and its nature. A ''worm'' on the model of the earth-serpent, it is fifty feet long, winged, and fire-breathing, as well as ''wrapped in flames'' as it hurtles coiling through the night sky. It is as beautiful as an aurora, but terrifyingly impersonal in its destructiveness, like fate itself.

All three monsters mark a contrast of increasing starkness to the generous humanness of the pagan Scandinavians, especially Hrothgar, Beowulf, and Wiglaf. Hrothgar's metaphysical problem, ''things change,'' is symbolized by these unexpected monsters. The human answer to this problem is provided by young Wiglaf as he sees the life of his dear king and kinsman threatened by the dragon. Before rushing to risk his own life with Beowulf, he states the value that lies behind the ritual of giving, behind everything human: ''The ties of kinship [fellowship, human solidarity] can never be ignored by a noble man.'' This is a thing that does not change, for a man who thinks rightly!

Beowulf the Hero

Many early scholars gave the year 340 A.D. as the date of Beowulf's death; a more recent Scandinavian historian even tells us where he is "probably" buried! This "historicity" may have been picked up from the early nineteenth century accounts of the poem by Sharon Turner, who had confused the hero Beowulf with a certain Boe whose life is related by the twelfth century Danish historian, Saxo Grammaticus. It is very doubtful that a real Beowulf, who played the role of a culture hero during the migration period and attracted to himself poetic accounts of great exploits (like King Arthur), ever really lived. Moreover, the datable events in the poem belong not to the fourth century but to the sixth, coincidentally the time when a real person behind the legend of Arthur may have lived. Whereas the stories of the Arthur legend make up the mythical Celtic history of Britain, those around Beowulf may be said to make up the mythical Germanic history of some of the tribes that came to invade Britain. Beowulf the hero is almost certainly the creation of a great associative imagination.

The first element of his name, Beow, seems to carry mythic implications. The poem opens with a "digression," apparently irrelevant to the main plot, on the story of Shield Shefing, founder of the Danish dynasty, and the magnificent ship-burial in which he is sent out to sea as mysteriously as he arrived in Denmark. The purpose of this evocation of a mythical past would seem to be to remove us to a symbolic distance where, as Aristotle says, "poetry is something more philosophical and of graver import than history." In this section Beowulf the Dane, distinct from Beowulf the Geat who is the hero of the poem, appears in the same genealogical relationship to his family (Sheaf, Shield, Beowulf I) as does the divine being Beow in Anglo-Saxon and some Old Norse lists of kings. Many years ago philological investigations showed that the name Beow and the Old English word for grain *beow* were cognate with (corresponded to) the Old Norse **beggw-*, a hypothetical form becoming Finnish Pekko, the name of a god who was said to promote the growth of barley. In each culture, then, "the conclusion which it is difficult to avoid is that the corn-spirit 'Barley' and the ancestor 'Barley' are one and the same. The relation is the same as that between King Sheaf [the father of Shield in *Beowulf*] and the worship of the sheaf: the worshipped corn-being gradually sinks into the background, and comes to be regarded as an epic figure, an early ancestor" (Axel Olrik, quoted in Chamber's *Introduction*, p. 87).

Chambers proceeds from this identification to show, through several steps, that both the Grendel story and the dragon story seem to be derived from ancient culture myths connected with a god of agriculture and fertility called "Beow." He adds that "the author would no doubt have been highly scandalized had he suspected that his pattern of a young prince was only a disguised heathen god" (pp. 291–304).

Though it may be important to be aware of some

identity of the hero through his name with the mythical ancestor Beow, it is perhaps even more significant that the hero's name is not Beow but Beowulf. This name was explained by Grimm as meaning "bee-wulf," that is, wolf or devourer of bees, a kenning (or metaphor) for woodpecker. While Grimm's etymology, bee-wolf, is usually accepted, the meaning he attached to the kenning is not: it is usually interpreted to mean "bear." Thus the hero's name is one of the key elements which ties in the first half of the story with a series of folklore analogues found throughout the world, even in Japan and among the Aztecs of Mexico; this folktale type is called the "Bear's Son Tale," because in many versions the hero is kin to a bear (as is Bjarki, "Little Bear," in the Old Norse *Hrolf Kraki's Saga*), or is raised by bears, or in some way partakes of the nature of a bear. Beowulf has the grip of thirty men and in the rage of battle slays his foes with a "bear-hug," though the poet makes no explicit connection, nor even mentions bears in the poem.

There is a third matter of importance to be discussed in connection with Beowulf's name. It was a standard practice among Germanic tribes to give sons names that alliterated with the names of their fathers, and often with the name of the tribe as well. This principle of name giving can be seen in operation in most of the families of the poem: Halfdane's sons were Heorogar, Hrothgar, and Halga the Good; Hrothgar's children were Hrothmund, Hrethric, and a daughter Freawaru (perhaps a term descriptive of character rather than a name), and he named his hall Heorot. But Beowulf, said to be of the Wagmunding clan and having as relatives Weohstan and Wiglaf, has a name which does not alliterate on W, nor does it alliterate with the name of his father Edgetheow. Therefore, it has been suggested that in the traditions upon which the poet drew there were originally two or even three persons behind this hero, perhaps each participating in one of the three adventures. The Swedish philologist Schück thought there might have been a Beow, a Wagmunding Wulf(–), and Edgetheow's unnamed son, all of whom the poet moulded into one hero participating in a connected sequence of fights. (This search for antecedents of the hero is not of particular concern to scholars today.)

The Fights with Grendel and his Mother

As mentioned above, the first part of *Beowulf* seems to be a highly sophisticated version of the ''Bear's Son Tale,'' which would make the first two fights generically related. A summary of the type, derived from about two hundred versions collected by the folklorist Panzer, is as follows:

> The hero, a young man of extraordinary strength, sets out on his adventures, accompanied by chosen followers. A great but aged king has built a ceremonial hall, which a demon has come to haunt by night. The king's elder sons and champions are

unable to quell him. The hero comes to the hall, and one by one his comrades fail to conquer the monster. Finally the hero himself succeeds in wounding the demon, who flees. Following the blood-stained trail, the hero finds the demon's den below the earth; it is usually protected by fire and water. He is let down by a rope and overcomes a number of supernatural foes in this underworld, including the demon and other demons or the original demon's mother. Occasionally he wins the battle only by using a magic sword found below, which he retains as a trophy. The hero is left treacherously in the lurch by his companions, whose duty it was to have drawn him up from the lair of the demon, but he succeeds in escaping nevertheless. In the later European versions there is usually a captive maiden whom the hero frees and by whom he is suitably rewarded. (See Chamber's *Introduction,* p. 62, and Klaeber, pp. xiii–xiv.)

Though deviations from the story in *Beowulf* have been put forth by some scholars as evidence that the poem belongs to a different folktale group, the parallels are obvious between the "Bear's Son Tale" and *Beowulf,* above all the connected sequence of fights first in the aged king's hall then in the demonic cave. (It should be noted that in *Beowulf* the "cave" is a demonic hall.)

That such stories were current in Scandinavia around 1250 A.D. is commonly demonstrated by three saga fights having points of similarity to Beowulf's, those of Grettir the Strong, of Orm, and of Bothvar Bjarki.

It seems reasonable to argue that these parallels have occurred through the use of the same or similar Germanic sources for both the Old English and the Old Norse accounts. Apparently two stories existed in the tradition (as we have it), one of the freeing of the Danish court from a monster by a brave warrior, and the other of a fight with two monsters in a cave. Eventually these stories were attached to various culture heroes, some of whom were undoubtedly historical, others probably not. For a fuller discussion of these Scandinavian analogues than I intend here, see Klaeber, pp. xiv-xx, and Chamber's *Introduction;* for English translations see Garmondsway and Simpson's *Beowulf and Its Analogues.* I shall only summarize the most relevant points of the Bjarki and Grettir fights.

The great achievement of Bothvar Bjarki, a warrior in the *Saga of Hrolf Kraki,* has a strong resemblance to Beowulf's fight with Grendel: he sets out on adventure and frees the king's court from a monster who haunts it. (The Danish king in the saga, Hrolf Kraki, appears in *Beowulf* as Hrothgar's nephew Hrothulf.) Bothvar, however, also redeems a coward, Hott, who, after drinking the monster's blood, becomes a champion second only to Bjarki. This feature, and an earlier parallel in Saxo Grammaticus where Bjarki has a companion drink bear's blood to become stronger, has led the Danish scholar Axel Olrik to oppose any suggestion of a connection between this saga and *Beowulf.* Chambers, Klaeber, and others, however, argue that the stories have enough in common for Bjarki's deeds to be considered seriously as an analogue to Beowulf's, and recently Robinson has suggested that in the Bjarki-Hott relationship there is conceivably "a remote echo of the interplay between Beowulf and Unferth" ("Elements of the Marvellous in the Characterization of Beowulf," *Old English Studies in Honour of John C. Pope,* edited by Robert B. Burlin and Edward B. Irving, Jr. [Toronto: University of Toronto Press, 1974], p. 131).

The *Saga of Grettir,* the story of the great Robin Hood of Icelandic outlaws, is a more important analogue. Grettir was a real person who was killed in 1031, but between his death and the compilation of the saga in the thirteenth century many folktale exploits had become attached to his name. One of these is the story of Glam, a huge and very solid ghost analogous in some ways to the demon Grendel, who haunts a certain farmhouse. Grettir comes to the rescue, and one night he waits alone for Glam's attack. Glam enters the hall, and they wrestle up and down its length. Finally Grettir overcomes the "ghost" and cuts off his head, but not before Glam has caught him in the shining glare of his eyes and cursed him in a way that later results in his death.

The other episode related to *Beowulf* is Grettir's underground adventure at Sandhaugar. This is a farm haunted by an ogress who has spirited away two men at Christmas. Again Grettir waits alone for the attack. When the ogress comes for him he fights unsuccessfully at first and is dragged to the edge of a gorge, but he manages to hack off the monster's arm before he is dragged down. Believing that the two missing men are below, he persuades a priest, Stein, to watch by a rope while he descends. Grettir goes down the rope, lands in water at the bottom, swims under the falls, and finds a cave in which a giant is sitting by a fire. The giant swings at him with a *hepti-sax* (a word found only here and, in its Old English form, at line 1457 in *Beowulf*), but Grettir avoids the blow and wounds the giant. Stein, seeing from above the blood-stained water in the pool, assumes that Grettir has been killed and goes home. "But Grettir let little space come between his blows until the giant lay dead." Afterwards he finds the bones of the two dead men in the cave, climbs up the rope, and leaves the bones in Stein's church.

It is argued by many scholars, who put perhaps too much weight on the uniquely occurring words *hepti-sax* in the *Saga of Grettir* and *hæft-mece* in *Beowulf,* that there is a very close connection indeed between these stories. The usual conclusion, however, is that they are both derived independently from one common Germanic source. Perhaps the combination of the two story-elements, the fight with the supernatural being in the hall and with the troll-wife and troll of the underwater cave, was the independent work of the poet himself in *Beowulf* and of the Icelandic author in the *Saga of Grettir*. But the fact that they occur in combination in so many of the "Bear's Son" tales would suggest that the totemic hero's double exorcism of demonic powers, first in a center of civilization and then in the shadowy otherworld itself, is either part of a very ancient oral tradition or else is a natural expression of the human fear of the unknown and the desire that its mysteries should be controlled.

The Fight with the Dragon

The dragon adventure, which some modern critics say is not far removed in kind from the other two fights, is found many times over in Germanic literature. Two main variations of the traditional dragon fight can be distinguished: the Sigurd type (Sigemund in our poem), where a dragon is fought for his treasure, and the Thor type, where the dragon is fought to save the people and the hero loses his own life. Sometimes these types overlap, as in *The Hobbit;* of course in romantic literature and fairy tales the hero seldom dies. In some Scandinavian genealogies a hero, Frotho, who fights a dragon for treasure, occupies the place of Beowulf I in the poem, which leads some to suggest that the dragon fight was originally a feat of a Danish Beowulf who was identical with Frotho, and that the fight was later transferred to Beowulf the Geat. Frotho's fight is of the Sigurd type, however, while the Geatish Beowulf's fight is primarily of the Thor type (although his interest in the treasure lessens the value of this distinction of types).

While the folklorists' concern with kinds of dragon fight is useful for thinking about the poem, the most pressing question for the reader is, how real was the dragon meant to be? We tend to assume the abysmal ignorance of an age other than our own, and thus the naive answer would be a condescending affirmation of the Anglo-Saxon belief in dragons. And to be sure, the *Anglo-Saxon Chronicle* mentions dragons flying in A.D. 793, and one of the gnomic verses of *Maxims II* pronounces:

> The dragon shall dwell in the barrow,
> Old, proud of his treasures.

Nor did the dragons all vanish with the Renaissance; Chambers mentions the report of a dragon flying from Mount Pilatus as recently as 1649 (*Introduction*, p. 11 n), and when I was visiting in the Arctic, I was told not to make a loud noise when watching the looping, coiling curves of the Aurora Borealis, because if I drew attention to myself that flaming creature would "come down and get me"! But today on the whole sky-dragons have been supplanted in popular belief by aliens from farther away.

In any case the question of belief is not so simple as it appears on the surface: do you believe, yes or no? The anthropologist Levi-Strauss has argued that the "sauvage" or pre-scientific mind would draw the line of belief on a different axis from the modern scientific line between real and unreal. Aristotle defines reality in terms of hierarchies, and for him the most real things are symbolic truths. In that sense, the only sense that matters in the realms of poetry and other forms of "archaic" thought, of course dragons are real, as real as death, buried treasure, Satanic forces and the sin of pride, with which they are associated. Perhaps one can analyze dragons scientifically by saying that they are the projections of our fears upon the ribboning lights of the northern night sky or the half-seen creatures of the sea, but the point is, when these things are glimpsed and endowed with malevolence, our stomachs and pulses call them real, even today. That fiery dragon in *Beowulf* is fifty feet long, and angry!

In "Beowulf's Fight with the Dragon," *Review of English Studies,* n.s. 9 (1958), Kenneth Sisam gives a good blow-by-blow account of that fight, and Tolkien argues eloquently for the related symbolism of all three of Beowulf's fights in *"Beowulf:* The Monsters and the Critics," available in the anthologies. T. A. Shippey, using Propp's morphology of the folktale in quite a different line of argument, argues for the structural relationship of the three encounters in "The Fairy-Tale Structure of *Beowulf,"* *Notes and Queries,* 16 (1969), 2–11.

While Shippey concludes that the main plot of *Beowulf* follows the structure of the traditional fairy-tale, point by point, he observes that the magic that pervades such tales is notably absent:

> One insight that we gain into *Beowulf* [using Propp's methods of analysis] is that it is this magical element that the poet likes least, for he can be seen, not only disguising his hero's bear-nature and converting water-fall caves into submarine halls, but also trying to blot out the typical features of the magical object of search and the magic property that helps in the search. The poet's Christianity may have

something to do with this rationalization; but it seems more likely to come from the fact that he is an epic and elegaic poet, concerned above all with human problems and tragedies, wanting no fantasy to degrade his hero with easy assistance. *Beowulf* is a fairy-tale with all the magic removed, as far as possible—a paradox worth considering.

(pp. 10–11)

A powerful effect of this suppression of fairy-tale magic is to make the monsters more real: the two trolls are real cannibals and the dragon a real "jaws"-monster, but bigger than life and burning with a supernatural evil. If one can distinguish between fantasy and the supernatural, one begins to see just how different *Beowulf* is from a fairy-tale. A fairy-tale is not intended to be "believed in" in the same way that angelic and demonic forces are. While the monsters themselves are malevolent forms from folklore, the evil impulse, the demonic force that motivates their attack, is to be found in scriptural history. Scriptural history, while different in kind from the secular history in the poem, would command a similar respect for its "truth" from an audience sufficiently instructed to recognize it. (There will be more about this at the end of the chapter on Christianity.)

Like Thor's apocalyptic fight with the Midgard Serpent, Beowulf's fight with the dragon has been thought by some to symbolize the end of a "world" for the Geats, because once the hero-king is dead, the fierce Swedes are expected to descend upon the kingdom. This thesis impinges upon the historical matter which will be discussed in the next chapter.

II The Historical Sub-Plot

The Tribes and their Vendettas

The history in *Beowulf*, which makes up most of the famous digressions in the poem, is chiefly concerned with feuds. Dorothy Whitelock remarks that the historical Scandinavian feuds are

> referred to so frequently that it is obvious that the poet wishes them to be present in his hearers' thoughts as he tells his tale. The tragic stories of family strife within the Scylding dynasty, and of the wars fought by the kings of the Geats against the Swedes or Franks, attain almost to the position of sub-plots to the two parts of *Beowulf* respectively.
>
> (*The Audience of Beowulf*, p. 34)

While the main plot of *Beowulf*, abstracted from its setting, seems almost too simple, a modern reader finds these "sub-plots," the background against which the story is set, too complicated. The Scandinavian history in the poem seems difficult for us to grasp chiefly because of the poet's allusive method of referring to "off-stage" events as though they are well known to his audience.

But this is not such an insurmountable obstacle as it seems at first. Once one is clear about the tribal affiliations of the main rulers and warriors, then the events themselves become increasingly clear as well; the reconstructed chronology at the end of this chapter will help with this clarification. The genealogical chart which is appended will help to establish the relationships between main characters, and the maps, simplified from Klaeber, will give some idea of the geographical relationships of the tribes involved. It is worth taking some time to grasp these events and relationships, the historical "sub-plots" of the poem, because they can be the most confusing element even in a translation.

The four major tribes in *Beowulf* are the Geats, the Swedes, the Danes and the Heathobards. I shall discuss them in turn below (with references to the fifth main tribe, the Frisians, explained in the course of the discussion), and analyze their relation to the historical sub-plots.

The Geats

The most important Geatish characters in the poem are Hrethel, Hathcyn, Hygelac, Hygd, Beowulf and Wiglaf.

Documents other than Beowulf *that refer to Hygelac are Gregory of Tours'* History of the Franks, *the anonymous* Liber Historiae Francorum, *and the anonymous* Liber Monstrorum de Diversis Generibus.

The Geats are mentioned in the Old English poems "Widsith" and "Deor."

In a section of his *History of the Franks* which he

completed in 575, Gregory of Tours tells how "the Danes with their king whose name was Chlochilaicus, having crossed the sea with a fleet, came to Gaul [i.e. the Rhine Delta] and . . . laid waste a certain district of the kingdom of Theuderic [king of the Franks 511–534] and took prisoners." But when Theuderic heard of this, the story continues, he sent his son Theudebert with an army and a large show of weapons; the Franks killed Chlochilaicus and overcame his fleet in a naval battle. By remarkable insight the Danish scholar Grundtvig in 1815 identified this Chlochilaicus with the Hygelac of *Beowulf*. According to R. W. Chambers, this identification is "the most important discovery ever made in the study of *Beowulf*, and the foundation of our belief in the historic character of its episodes" (*Introduction*, p. 4n). Later Latin accounts, deriving partly from Gregory of Tours and partly from unidentified sources, give the king's name as Chochilaicus or Higlacus and his people as the Goti or Geti. The raid is mentioned four times in *Beowulf*:

1202–14a	The Frisians, neighbors of the Hetware, and the Franks are described as enemies. Hygelac is slain.
2354–68	Beowulf escapes from the battle after slaying many of the Hetware (a tribe living hear the mouth of the Rhine).
2500–08	Beowulf kills Dayraven, a Frankish warrior in the service of the Frisian king.

2910b–21   When Beowulf dies, strife is expected from
the Franks, Frisians and Hetware because
of Hygelac's raid of over half a century
before.

The date given for this historical raid by the most
recent scholarship is 523 A.D. [*] Those who think that
the poem is at least partly about the fall c ᵗhe Geats
argue that there is no confirmation of the existence
of a king of the Gautar after Hygelac.

Although Hygelac was established as a historical
king early in the history of *Beowulf* scholarship, the
identity of his people, the Geats, has long been a
matter of controversy. The main discussion has been
whether they are the Jutes or the Old Norse Gautar
(modern Swedish Götar), but they have also been
identified as the long-extinct Thracian tribe, the
Getae. The main arguments for each of these three
theories are as follows.

1. *Jutes.* One of the most powerful pro-Jutish
arguments was that the Swedish King Ottar Vendel-
kraka (Othere in *Beowulf*) was traditionally nick-
named "The Vendel Crow" because he had been
struck down in battle and buried in Vendel in Jut-
land. This has been proven false by local traditions
and by archaeology, both of which place Ottar's
grave at Vendel in Uppland, Sweden. Ottar's Swedish
burial suggests that the Jutes had little to do with
his death, and thus that they are not to be identified
with the Geats of *Beowulf*.

[*] G. Storms, "The Significance of Hygelac's Raid," *Nottingham
Medieval Studies*, XIV (1970), 3–26.

2. *Gautar.* The theory most commonly accepted
is that the Geats are the Gautar, with which their
name corresponds etymologically (Germanic *au* corresponds to Old English *ea*). Recently Swedish historians have claimed that the Gautar tribe extended over
more of what is now southwest Sweden (Västergötland) than was previously thought. Along with the
Danes and the Swedes, the Gautar appear to have
been one of the three most important tribes of
the North.

3. *Getae.* Jane Acomb Leake's theory in *The
Geats of Beowulf* (Madison: University of Wisconsin
Press, 1967) that the Geats were the Getae is based
on Classical and Patristic legends of the barbaric
North. The name Getae, once identified with an
outlying barbaric tribe of ancient Thrace, was shifted
first to the Scythians, then to the Scandinavians;
ultimately it became a poetic term corresponding to
"Goth," which in Latin literature was associated
with much of the same sense of savagery and grandeur
as it was in the Gothic Movement of eighteenth century England, and the name was anglicized, says
Leake, to "Geat" by the *Beowulf* poet. This purely
literary derivation of the Geats, by which Leake
claims to establish that both the tribe and their king
Hygelac were "an unreal people," has been legiti-
mately criticized on philological grounds. What has
not been observed is that such an established literary
use of a similar name would provide the *Beowulf*
poet with a feeling that there was an authoritative
precedent for his poetic presentation of the more
precisely historical Geats.

Some attempts have been made to establish historical connections between the Geats of *Beowulf* (and of "Widsith" and "Deor") and material remains in Scandinavia and England. The most interesting of these is Charles Green's proposal (suggested first by Sune Lindqvist) in *Sutton Hoo* (London, 1963, second ed. 1968) that Wiglaf, Beowulf's relative who survives him and to whom he entrusts his people, is an ancestor of the East Anglian king for whom the great Sutton Hoo cenotaph was built. Both the method of ship burial and several of the Sutton Hoo treasures have a close connection with the area of Uppland, Sweden, and the name of Wiglaf's father, Weohstan, who slew the brother of the king who ruled Sweden at Beowulf's death, may correspond with the name Wehha in the East Anglian dynasty. It is possible that Wiglaf, when entrusted with the care of the Geats yet threatened with Swedish vengeance for his father's deed, thought discretion the better part of valor and established the new gift-throne of his people (of those who were left and wished to follow him) in that beckoning land across the sea. This speculation makes a pleasant postscript to *Beowulf,* and even offers a suggestion about why a Scandinavian hero poem came to be composed in England. But there is no way of substantiating it as truth, and in *Beowulf: Swedes and Geats* (London: Viking Society for Northern Research, 1972) R. T. Farrell objects to it strongly as unhistorical.

Related to this speculation, however, is a similar one concerning the fate of Hengest after the destruction of Finnsburg. (If there is anything in this theory, it gives the Jutes an important place in *Beowulf,* even though they are not the Geats.) Hengest, the mercenary warrior in allegiance with the Danes, who is the key figure in the Finnsburg episode, may have found it inadvisable to return with his following to the land of the Danes after the fight in which the Danish prince was killed, a fight for which the Jutes (if one may translate *Eotenas* thus, not merely as "enemies") were in some sense responsible. This tale of the Finnsburg fights, told in Hrothgar's court, could well refer to historical events occurring in the previous century. That would make the time coincide approximately with the traditional date, 449 A.D., of the expedition of the Angles, Saxons and Jutes under the leadership of the Jutish brothers, Hengist and Horsa, to aid the British king Vortigern; according to Bede, this expedition led to the establishment of the first of the Germanic settlements in England— after Hengist broke his oath to serve the king and established his own rule.

It must be remembered that such associations of characters in the poem with the Germanic settlement of England are based on the most tenuous similarities of name, date and character attributes; they are interesting, and just possible, but must never be taken as fact.

The Swedes

The most important Swedish characters in Beowulf *are in the sub-plot only: Ongentheow, Ohthere,*

Onla, Eadmund and Eadgils. They are mentioned in Old Norse in the verse Ynglingatal *and the prose* Ynglinga Saga *and in early Latin histories of Denmark.*

The struggles for succession between the members of the Swedish royal family, the Shilfings, can be reconstructed through allusions in *Beowulf,* the *Ynglingatal,* and the *Ynglinga Saga.* Ongentheow, king of the Swedes and Hathcyn's mortal foe, is called Angantyr in the very early Norse poem, the *Ynglingatal,* while the later prose account of the early kings, the *Ynglinga Saga,* tells of the son and grandson of Angantyr, Ottar (Old English Ohthere) and Athils (Old English Eadgils) as well as of Angantyr himself. Their existence has been further confirmed by the identification of their graves among the royal mounds in northern Sweden. Onla (Onela in Old English) is called Ali or Anle the Mad in Norse sources, and is thought by some to be the historical figure behind—far behind—Hamlet. * The *Ynglinga Saga* describes the final struggle between Onla and Eadgils as a winter battle on ice on one of the great Swedish lakes; this corresponds to the account in lines 2391–96 of the poem, and suggests that "the wide ocean" of 2395 is really an inland "sea."

Kemp Malone "proves" this idea with philology. Perhaps a more convincing way of linking Hamlet to Beowulf's story is as follows: The Scandinavian Hamlet is named Amlothi in various sources. In his *History of the Danes*, Saxo Grammaticus (d. ca. 1220) implicitly makes him Hrothgar's great-grandson by the following line of descent: Hrothgar (Latin Ro) → Hrethric (Latin Roricus) → Gerutha (Shakespeare's Gertrude) → Amlothi (Hamlet).

At the end of *Beowulf* there is an obscure prophecy which has been interpreted to indicate the poet's knowledge of the fall of the Geats after the death of their king. The messenger who has been sent from the scene of the dragon fight to carry the news of Beowulf's death announces that now he fears war from the Swedes, the Franks, and other tribes that have been antagonistic in the past. Swedish historians claim that Sweden is the oldest political entity in Europe, and that the subjugation of the Gautar by the Swedes some time around the middle of the first millennium A.D. marks the establishment of the kingdom of Sweden. In *Beowulf* the Swedes seem to be the Geats' most persistent enemies. Arguing over the question of whether the Swedes did conquer the Geats after Beowulf's death is fruitless—we are not told this in the poem; we are only told of the messenger's fears. But if those fears came true and the Swedes did sweep down to conquer, then the poem may well herald the birth of the Swedish state. Again, as with the destinies of Wiglaf and Hengest, the poet may be alluding to history of which his audience has fuller knowledge than we do; on the other hand, we may be manufacturing history on the basis of what we see as hints in the poem.

The nationalistic interest that leads some Swedish historians to take *Beowulf* very seriously as a document of their earliest history does not inspire the most objective approach. The following summary of the Scylfing-Geatish struggles in *Beowulf* is translated from Alf Henrickson's two volume *Svensk Historia* published in 1966:

The poem *Beowulf* is about saga-like exploits that
the Geatish hero Beowulf performed against trolls
and dragons in Denmark and at home, and intro-
duced into the saga there are some poetic accounts
of disputes between the Swedes and the Geats.
According to the poem the [Geatish] king, Hathcyn,
and his brother, Hygelac, went to the country of the
Swedes where they kidnapped the queen. The king
of the Swedes, Ongentheow, soon succeeded in
killing Hathcyn and setting his wife free, but he in
turn was struck down and killed by Hygelac, and was
succeeded then by his son Ohtere, who reigned
peacefully over the Swedes for a time. When Ohtere
died his brother Onla succeeded him instead of
his sons Eadgils and Eanmund, who then sought
help from the Geats against their uncle. The Geats'
young king, Heardred, aided them gladly, but Onla
became incensed and resolved to fight against the
Geats; he succeeded in killing Heardred and Eanmund, but Eadgils was not wounded. Eadgils went
to Beowulf, the Geats' new king, and together they
undertook to fight against Onla, who died in the
battle. Then Eadgils became the king of the Swedes.

The account of the fighting Swedish and Geatish
countries with their strange names is rather unclear,
and one ought not to expect anything else from an
Anglo-Saxon heroic poem. What one can say about
the story of Beowulf as a source for early Swedish
history is that it confirms from an unexpected source
some names in Snorri's lists of kings. There is a
patriotic controversy, still unresolved, about whether
the [tribal name] Geatas means the Götar or the
Jutes; this continues to be a matter for discussion

among scholars, who are nowadays the only persons who retain an interest in the problem for its own sake. The most intriguing discussion of the subject comes from the Götar side, which says that *Beowulf* tells of the battles that ended with Västergötland becoming a part of the country of the Swedes; this took place around the year 500 A.D., and the catastrophe for the 'West Geats' occurred after the brave Beowulf had died and perhaps been buried in a mound at Skalund beside Lake Väner.

Arguing against the assumption that there was a fall of the Geats around 550 A.D., R. T. Farrel says in *Beowulf: Swedes and Geats* (London: Viking Society for Northern Research, 1971):

A realistic view, based on such scant evidence as we have, is that the *Gautar* were gradually dominated by the *Svear*, and that they were gradually subsumed into the larger kingdom of Sweden, while maintaining their cultural identity in many respects. This process was not completed until well after A.D. 1000. There is no evidence for a destruction of the *Gautar* as a people at any time. This account does not contradict what is said in *Beowulf* about the two powers. They engage in a series of battles, with victories on either side. Quite naturally, once they have lost a strong ruler, the Geats fear incursions from without—but there is no mention of tribal destruction in *Beowulf,* and none in history.

(pp. 42–43)

Such arguments put forth by Farrell and others take

some of the force out of the thesis that *Beowulf* is in some way about "the rise and fall of nations."

The Danes and the Heathobards

The most important Danes in the poem are Shield, Hrothgar, Hrothulf, Wealtheow (though she is actually a foreigner), Freawaru, Hrothmund and Hrethric. Outside references to Shield, Hrothulf and Hrethric, in particular, are many; among these the Old English poem "Widsith," the Old Norse prose Saga of Hrolf Kraki, and the Old Norse eddic lays of "Helgi Hundingsbana" are mentioned below.

The Heathobards important in the poem are Froda and his son Ingeld. In English sources Ingeld is mentioned in the Old English "Widsith" and in a letter in Latin from Alcuin to the Bishop of Lindisfarne in Northumbria.

It has been suggested that while the *Beowulf* poet actually knew Geatish and Swedish history, his knowledge of Danish heroic traditions was based mainly on poetic sources. Certainly Shield Shefing is a mythical figure, and the poet's accounts of Danish affairs generally seem far less true to history than his accounts of the Swedish-Geatish wars. Kenneth Sisam *(The Structure of Beowulf)* is not alone in believing that far too much historical detail has been built up by scholars on the shaky basis of hints in *Beowulf* and other later works, though he surely goes too far in denying the allusive techniques in the poem. In any case, the course of events which seems to be suggested in *Beowulf* and "Widsith" as taking place in the Danish court in the early sixth century may be summarized as follows.

Froda, the king of the Heathobards, killed Halfdane, so Halfdane's sons were honor bound to kill Froda in return. To prevent further vengeance after this slaying, Hrothgar has his daughter Freawaru marry Froda's son Ingeld, but this does not prove effective. "Cooler will be his love for his queen" (line 2066) when Ingeld is urged on by his father's thanes to avenge him. Apparently he succeeds in burning down Heorot, but the Danes win the ensuing battle. At this point we must take up the story from Scandinavian sources. After Hrothgar's death, Hrothulf, son of Halga, comes to the throne instead of Hrothgar's own sons. Whether Hrothulf becomes king by fair means or foul is unclear; genealogies, chronicle accounts, poetry and saga suggest that at the center of this affair may be one of the more interesting unsolved murder mysteries of ancient times. On the other hand, since succession to the throne was often determined by election (among suitably royal candidates), it is perfectly possible that the historical Hrothulf was not the villain that he is often made out to be by *Beowulf* scholars—and apparently by the poet himself. In later traditions Hrothulf is immortalized in the saga bearing his name as the famous hero-king Hrolf Kraki, a sort of Danish King Arthur.

Ingeld is mentioned twice in English sources other than *Beowulf*. In "Widsith," Hrothgar and Hrothulf are said to have kept friendship together for a very

long time after they routed Ingeld's warriors at
Heorot. In a letter to the monks at Lindisfarne, Alcuin
warns them to guard themselves against secular literature, for "what does Ingeld have to do with Christ?"
Both references are as likely to be to a purely fictional
saga hero as to a historical figure. Ingeld's people,
the Heathobards, have not been firmly identified
with any known tribe, but they seem to have been a
seafaring people living on the shores of the Baltic.
In the Old Norse lays of "Helgi Hundingsbana,"
there is a Baltic warrior Hothbroddr who is an enemy
of Helgi (Halga, brother of Hrothgar, in *Beowulf*);
both Hothbroddr's name and his relationships suggest that he may be a personification of the Heatho-
bard tribe.

The Gift Hall of the Danes and the Monster's Mere

The traditional capital of the Shielding dynasty
was Hleiðra, situated southwest of Roskilde on the
island of Zealand, in Denmark. There is nothing
there now but the tiny village whose name, Lejre, is
the modernized form of Hleiðra. The German scholar
Sarrazin made a pilgrimage to the village and claimed
that he recognized geographical features described in
Beowulf; others, including Klaeber, have failed to see
any significant resemblance between the place and
the descriptions in the poem. The example of Chau-
cer demonstrates how unconcerned an early poet
writing about another land may be with native features: in a poem set in ancient Troy he has his heroine

Criseyde living in a typical fourteenth-century English house. Likewise, it is probable that the *Beowulf* poet described Hrothgar's magnificent hall on the basis of architecture with which he was familiar in England; it appears to be a highly ornamented Anglo-Saxon hall with a floor of variegated colors (Roman paving has been suggested, but I favor painted wood) and gilding on the gabled roof. The poet may have based his descriptions of the court on some such great royal establishment as that recently excavated at Yeavering in the north of England (Northumbria), where there once stood halls from sixty to one hundred feet long. Though the name Heorot alliterates with the name of the Shielding court, Hleiðra, it is not found in Scandinavian traditions of the Shieldings. It is found, however, as the name of a village in Northumbria, Hart, near Hartlepool, where a small church established in the time of Bede still exists, and the name is suitable for a hall with branching ''horns'' or gable beams like the reconstructed Danish hall and the stylized illustration from the *Book of Kells* that illustrate the text. The same kind of building, ''high and wide-gabled'' (line 82) was considered suitable to house princes, idols, or crosses, and was sometimes built in cathedral-like dimensions. Exactly the same phrase, ''high and wide-gabled,'' is used to describe the Temple of Solomon in the Old English poem *Andreas,* which was also envisioned by that poet as a huge timbered hall typical of north-west Europe.

The great locodescriptive poetry in *Beowulf* about Grendel's mere, lines 1357–76, contains features

reminiscent of a *visio Pauli*, the visions of Paul in
the desert, with elements of the Christian Hell in
a dark and watery wasteland; just such a landscape
is evoked in the seventeenth "Blickling Homily."
Despite the derivative character of such set descriptions of a demonic landscape, however, it is possible
that the poet was also influenced by native Celtic
traditions or even material remains such as those in
the area of Hadrian's Wall (near Yeavering) for
Grendel's pool, as well as by Christian tradition.
Along the wall are various wells and springs dedi-
cated by the Roman legions to the original Celtic
gods and goddesses of the area, such as Coventina
(who does not fit into the Roman pantheon in any
way) and Maponus ("Son of the Mother," related
to the Welsh Mabon of the *Mabinogion*). Such supernatural beings and the waters sacred to them are part
of the lore of north-west Europe, but those native
gods long established in the British Isles would have
the added advantage of being categorized as demons
hostile to God by the Christian church.

Soon after the first edition of this book was published,
excavations at Lejre (Hleiðra) uncovered evidence of a
tenth-century hall some 160 feet long, and on the same
site an earlier hall of ca. 660 AD almost as huge. Now
further buildings are being discovered. Scandinavian
sources associate this site with the ruling dynasty called the
Shieldings (Scyldingas) in *Beowulf*, and it is possible, some
would say likely, that the poet would have known about one
or another of these Danish halls, the largest yet discovered
in Northern Europe.

35

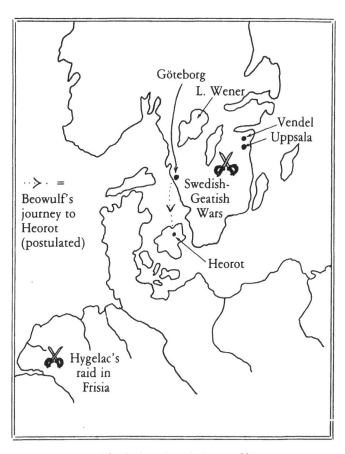

Göteborg

L. Wener

Vendel

Uppsala

Swedish-
Geatish
Wars

··>· =
Beowulf's
journey to
Heorot
(postulated)

Heorot

Hygelac's
raid in
Frisia

Physical settings in *Beowulf*

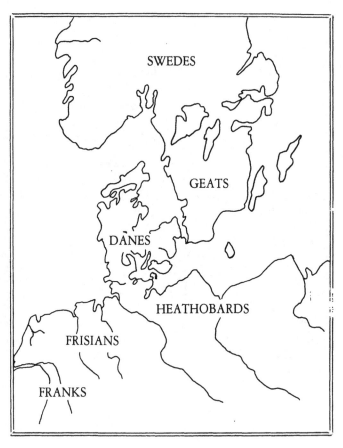

The Main Tribes in *Beowulf*

Modern Scandinavia

38

Charts

Beowulf: A Reconstructed Chronology

This chart is based on Klaeber's reconstruction, especially p. xiv. As he admits, the only date verifiable by outside evidence is Hygelac's death, c. 521; the other dates, calculated from Hygelac's death, are guesses based on legends, contemporary accounts, and archaeological finds. Beowulf and Wiglaf (but not Wiglaf's father Weohstan, ON Vésteinn) represent the only family group mentioned below whose existence is not in some way confirmed by evidence outside the poem.

Key to tribes (alternative tribal names in *Beowulf* are in parentheses):

- D: Danes (Dene, Beorht-Dene, Gar-Dene, Hring-Dene, East-Dene, Norð-Dene, Suð-Dene, West-Dene, Healf-Dene, Scyldingas, Ar-Scyldingas, Here-Scyldingas, Sige-Scyldingas, Þeod-Scyldingas, Ingwine).
- F: Frisians (Fresan, Frysan).
- G: Geats (Geatas, Guð-Geatas, Sæ-Geatas, Weder-Geatas, Wederas, Hreðlingas).
- HB: Heathobards (Heaðobeardan).
- S: Swedes (Sweon, Scylfingas, Guð-Scylfingas, Heoðo-Scylfingas).

Date	Tribes	Event
495	G, S(?)	Beowulf born, son of Edgetheow (a Swede?), grandson of Hrethel.
498	HB, D	Froda kills Halfdane; Froda's son Ingeld born.
499	HB, D	Heorogar, Hrothgar, and Halga kill Froda.
502	G	Hathcyn accidentally kills his brother Herebeald.
503	G	Their father Hrethel dies of grief; Hathcyn becomes king of the Geats.
503	G, S	Swedes attack Geats at Sorrowhill: FIRST SWEDISH-GEATISH WAR begins.
510	G, S	Hathcyn and Hygelac attack the Swedes and abduct their queen. In the ensuing BATTLE OF RAVENSWOOD, both Hathcyn of the Geats and Ongentheow, the Swedish king, are killed. Hathcyn's brother Hygelac becomes king of the Geats and Ohthere king of the Swedes.
515	G, D	Beowulf cleanses Heorot of monsters.
518	HB, D	Hrothgar, who with his brothers Heorogar and Halga had killed king Froda in vengeance for their father Halfdane's death, gives his daughter Freawaru in marriage to Froda's son Ingeld to forestall a renewal of the feud.
520	HB, D	Ingeld attacks after all, burns down Heorot, but is then defeated by Hrothgar and Hrothulf.
521	G, F	Hygelac of the Geats is killed in his ill-fated Frisian raid; Beowulf escapes by swim-

ming after killing Dayraven, perhaps the slayer of Hygelac. Heardred becomes king of the Geats with Beowulf acting as regent.

525 D   Hrothgar dies; his nephew Hrothulf comes to (usurps?) the throne.

532 G, S   SECOND SWEDISH-GEATISH WAR begins.

533 G, S   Death of the Swedish king Ohtere (Ottar Vendel-Crow, buried at Vendel in Uppland, Sweden). His brother Onla seizes the throne, while his sons Eanmund and Eadgils seek refuge in the Geatish court. Onla attacks the Geats, kills their young king Heardred; Beowulf (by Onla's permission?) becomes king of the Geats. In the battle Eanmund is killed by Weohstan, Onla's retainer. Weohstan is the father of Wiglaf, who is Beowulf's only surviving relative, his most loyal retainer, and becomes king of the Geats when Beowulf dies. Eadgil's desire to avenge his brother's death (a family feud rather than an element in the national wars) would cause his enmity not only toward Weohstan but, in case of Weohstan's death, toward his son Wiglaf as well.

535 G, S   Beowulf supports Eadgils in war against Onla.

(583) G   This date is a poetic fiction; note date of Beowulf's birth. Beowulf dies in battle with a fire-dragon. Wiglaf succeeds him as king of the Geats. THIRD SWEDISH-GEATISH WAR begins?

575 S   Eadgils is laid in a mound at Old Uppsala.

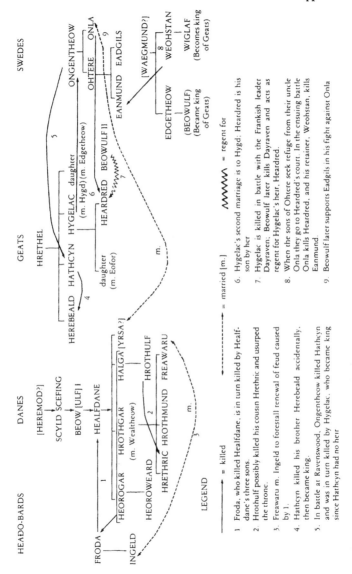

41

SWEDES

GEATS

DANES

HEADO-BARDS

LEGEND

→ = killed

┄┄→ = married [m.]

∿∿∿∿ = regent for

1 Froda, who killed Healfdane, is in turn killed by Healf-dane's three sons.

2 Hrothulf possibly killed his cousin Hrethric and usurped the throne.

3 Freawaru m. Ingeld to forestall renewal of feud caused by 1.

4 Hæthcyn killed his brother Herebeald accidentally, then became king.

5 In battle at Ravenswood, Ongentheow killed Hæthcyn and was in turn killed by Hygelac, who became king since Hæthcyn had no heir.

6 Hygelac's second marriage is to Hygd; Heardred is his son by her

7 Hygelac is killed in battle with the Frankish leader Dayraven; Beowulf later kills Dayraven and acts as regent for Hygelac's heir, Heardred.

8 When the sons of Ohtere seek refuge from their uncle Onla they go to Heardred's court. In the ensuing battle Onla kills Heardred, and his retainer, Weohstan, kills Eanmund.

9 Beowulf later supports Eadgils in his fight against Onla

III The Pagan-Christian "Problem" in *Beowulf*

The Christian "Coloring"

The Christian allusions in *Beowulf* have puzzled and often distressed commentators for well over a century. The early question about the Christianity was, what was it doing in a good pagan poem? From the time that Klaeber showed that it was integral to the poem, the question has shifted: what added meaning or message does it give the poem? Above all, does it make *Beowulf* an allegory? As my own opinion is that it emphatically does not, the reader is warned that my discussions of the allegorical interpretations will be highly critical.

Since the main subject matter of *Beowulf* is the drama of a Scandinavian hero in a pre-Christian age, there appears to be a tension in the poem between the passages that allude specifically to pagan customs, and those that allude to Christian doctrines. In the excerpt from *The Heroic Age* in Nicholson (a collection I shall draw on throughout this chapter), H. M. Chadwick lists the following as typical of the "heathen" elements in the poem:

The funeral ship in v. 27 ff., the offerings at the shrines in v. 175 f., the observation of the omens in v. 204 and the curious reference to hanging in v. 2444 ff. (cf. v. 2939 ff.), probably also the use of the boar on helmets (vv. 303 f., 1111 f., 1286, 1451 ff., 2152) and the burial of the treasure (v. 2233 ff.), together with the curse imprecated on the person who should disturb it (v. 3069 ff.). But most important of all are the descriptions of the disposal of the dead by cremation in vv. 1108 ff., 2124 ff., 3137 ff.

(p. 29)

One may add to this list the references to *wyrd* and such gnomic wisdom as that about avenging a friend (lines 1384-85) and achieving worldly glory, which for the atheling is "afterwards best" (1386-89). The poet, who is telling a tale set in a pre-Christian age, includes the rituals that reveal his protagonists' sense of the supernatural and the sayings that reveal their secular morality, even though these may run counter to his own. But the rituals themselves seem "cleaned up," with the more overtly sensational pagan elements removed. To see that the poet is telling of noble pagans, one need only compare the stately funerals of Shield and Beowulf with the Arab Ibn Fadlan's critical eye-witness account of a Rus chieftain's funeral. (Michael Crichton combined this historical event with the plot of *Beowulf* in a novel that was made into the movie *The Thirteenth Warrior*). The poet condemns as heathen and reprehensible only the Danish sacrifice at lines 175-188.

The Christian allusions are similarly restrained, however. Blackburn, whose 1897 article is included also in the Nicholson anthology, furnishes a long list of the passages and allusions that he sees as Christian. These contain no references to matters of specific Christian dogma such as angels, saints, Christ, the Cross, etc., only references to Old Testament events, to God, to judgment and damnation, and expressions of disapproval of heathen practices. As Clark Hall said, "A pious Jew would have no difficulty in assenting to them all."

The Christian element in *Beowulf* may well be what saved it from extinction during the later Anglo-Saxon period, when it was preserved in a monastic library. Yet it was just this element that for years incensed Germanic scholars against the "Christian redactor," who, they felt, had adulterated a noble pagan poem with interpolations of moralizing Christian matter that was "potentially of no value" (Henry Bradley in the *Encyclopedia Britannica*, 1910 ed.). On the whole these early scholars suggested that the "moralizing Christianity" was inserted in the poem not long after Christianity came to England, to reclaim the poem from its heathen past. But Chambers points out that modifications by a newly converted Christian or a Christian in a newly converted culture would have been emphatically Christian instead of mildly so; it would have been as easy to allude to the Trinity or the Cross as to the Lord of Hosts or the King of Glory (*Introduction*, pp. 125–127). Klaeber first showed how the "Christian element" was so inextricably fused with the rest of the poem that it could not be explained as the work of a Christian interpolator attempting to modify a completely pagan poem. Yet despite his view that "the narrative derived a superior dignity from suggesting the most exalted hero-life known to Christians" (p. 1i), Klaeber's basically pagan Germanic orientation toward the problem is shown by the title he chose for his discussion of it (following Blackburn), "The Christian Coloring."

The Fusion of Pagan and Christian Elements

Tolkien's approach in his lecture to this aspect of the poem, as to others, marks a complete break in the traditional scholarship (Nicholson anthology, pp. 51–103). He says that the poet's problem was not to give the pagan material with which he was working a Christian "color," but to avoid any obvious allusions to Christianity in a poem set in a world that was "heathen—heathen, noble and hopeless." The poet is writing sympathetically of a past heroic age, Tolkien says, but from a Christian perspective. His sympathy for the history of his race is seen in his *pietas,* "which treasures the memory of man's struggles in the dark past, man fallen and not yet saved, disgraced but not dethroned . . ." (p. 74). It is this very combination of Christianity and *pietas* that makes the poem a heroic elegy, a poem about a pre-

Christian past that is in many respects great and honorable, but doomed.

Marie Padgett Hamilton, in her article in the Nicholson anthology (pp. 105–135), attempts to explain this position in terms of St. Augustine's historical vision of the "Two Cities," in which all earthly societies are scenes of the eternal struggle between the representatives of the City of the Reprobate, who are doomed, and the citizens of the Celestial City. Charles Donahue, in "*Beowulf,* Ireland, and the Natural Good," *Traditio,* 7 (1949–51), 263–277, takes this a step farther and solves some difficulties by proposing that the good people in *Beowulf* "seem to belong neither to the City of the elect nor to that of the reprobate. They belong rather to what we might call a third city, a city which without supernatural hope fights a brave and losing fight against the forces of evil" (pp. 265–266). It is important to this interpretation and in keeping with Augustinian doctrine that, while Beowulf's soul is judged (lines 2819–20) and possibly accepted (Heaven swallows the smoke rising from his pyre, 3155), there remains an ambiguity about his ultimate destiny or that of any of the just men in the poem.

Ignoring these eschatological problems of the destiny of the just man under the "Old Law" before the revelation, Allen Cabaniss interprets the fight with Grendel's mother as an allegory of the rite of baptism ("*Beowulf* and the Liturgy" in the Nicholson anthology, pp. 223–232). In order to see how inextricably fused the two separate backgrounds of the poem are, I shall list below the seven points used by Cabaniss as proof for his argument, with a parallel list showing how the section about the fight with Grendel's mother could equally well stem from a tradition representing a pagan initiation rite.

"Thus, in succession of ideas and motifs, there is a significant parallel between Beowulf's adventure and Christ's death, harrowing of hell, and resurrection," says Cabaniss. He then proceeds to show how the same complex of ideas he finds connected with the episode of the mere—the harrowing of Hell, the deluge, and the creation—occur in the rites associated with Christian baptism.

In the same succession of ideas and motifs, however, there is a significant parallel between Beowulf's adventure and those of other Germanic heroes. This kind of comparative study of rituals dramatically poses the question of the ultimate sources of tradition. It is known that there were cave cults in western Europe from very early times, and it is possible that the "Bear's Son" tale or the "Fairy of the Mine" tale, as Klaeber prefers to call it, springs from a traditional ritual of death and rebirth, of the hero who descends on behalf of his tribe to the "other world" to confront a "dead" giant or seeress, sometimes having to fight the creature, and who comes away with some trophy representing wisdom or power. These stories are frequent in Norse literature,

(text continues on p. 54)

CHRISTIAN

1. The poet identifies the mere as Hell (852, 1274), an identification "perhaps strengthened by the statements that it is a water weirdly aflame (1365 f.), reminiscent of the Apocalyptic Lake which 'burneth with fire and brimstone: which is the second death'; and that it is a habitation of sea-monsters and sea-worms (1425–30, 1510–12; cf. Mark 9:44, 46, 48; Isaiah 66:24)."

2. "Beowulf prepares for his descent as though for death. As he girds himself, the hero mourns not at all for life (1442); as he addresses Hrothgar, he gives directions in the event of his dying (1477 f.). The parallel with Christ is even more striking as Beowulf magnanimously forgives his enemy Unferth just before the plunge into the fen-depths (1488–90; Cf. Luke 23:34).

3. "The descent itself is depicted as a victorious military campaign against the powers below (1441–71; cf. Colossians 2:15; I Corinthians 2:8; Revelations 1:18; 19:15; Psalm 24:7–10.)"

PAGAN

1. A pagan Germanic land of the dead called Hel and ruled by a goddess of the same name (see line 852 in this context) is the source for our English word "Hell." The approach to this land (or escape from it) is usually made difficult by a barrier of water, fire, or both. The "hall of the dead" in this land is wattled with worms (serpents).

2. This is paralleled in other tales of the "Bear's Son" group where the hero prepares to descend to confront the "the fairy in the mine." Any such descent must be in some sort a mimetic death. The theme of forgiveness, however, does seem specifically Christian, though in folksongs the dead often desire to break all ties of either love or spite with the living. Moreover, Unferth was Beowulf's "enemy" only in the verbal battle of lines 499–606, a *nith*-battle of a kind frequent in early Scandinavian literature. When this verbal battle is concluded, the enmity from which it arose is ideally forgotten.

3. "A victorious campaign"—so are many of the Norse battles of the Gods against the Giants, though in the end the Giants win. In some of the sagas, moreover, the hero must struggle with a dead man/giant/witch of the cave and subdue his antagonist in order to win the trophy of power

4. "At the moment of victory a beam of preternatural light penetrates the dismal scene beneath the waters and brightens it (1570–2; cf. Isaiah 4:2; Luke 1:78 f.)."

5. "In the meanwhile back on the edge of the mere, all the onlookers, except Beowulf's own faithful Geats, supposing that the hero has been killed, give up the vigil at the ninth hour of the day (1594–1602). It will be recalled immediately and inevitably that it was at the very same hour that Christ, abandoned by all but the most faithful few, died on the cross (Matthew 27:26; Mark 15:34, 37; Luke 23: 44–46)."

6. "The returning champion brings with him trophies of his victory (1612–15; Cf. Colossians 2:15)."

or knowledge and his return to the "normal" world. See the discussion of Grettir's fight in Chapter 1.

4. This also has analogues in folk-tales (as Klaeber notes), but here and in the light from the golden banner of the dead dragon's cave (2767) the light motif seems to be connected with the "limb" motif, on the one hand, and to be functioning in some symbolically Christian way, on the other hand.

5. Time measured in nines seems to be a typical feature of the Norse journey to the supernatural world: Odin hung on the tree for nine days and nine nights; Njorthr had to wait an equivalent amount of time for his Giantess bride, etc. Nevertheless, there is, to my knowledge, no Norse parallel so close as the Biblical one. On the other hand, Beowulf does not die; his antagonist does.

6. This seems to me more Germanic than Biblical. Both Odin and Sigurd make the pseudo-death journey in various forms in order to obtain "runes," i.e., supernatural knowledge. Beowulf returns to Heorot with a rune-engraved sword. The preserved head of a dead man is a common source of information about the future in Irish saga, and

7. ''Finally, there is a suggestion of winter's end and springtime's burgeoning as Beowulf comes up in triumph (1608–11), which, although not strictly Biblical, is one of the most ancient of Easter themes.''

PAGAN *(cont.)*

Odin has the preserved head of Mimur, who talks
more when dead than he did when alive. Presum-
ably the head of Grendel is, like the rune-sword,
an ''objective correlative'' for the power or wisdom gained by Beowulf in his journey below, and
not merely a grisly relic.

7. No comment needed.

as in epics. While it is true that the descent story in particular is easily adaptable to a Christian interpretation, I am not convinced that the *Beowulf* poet was centrally concerned with setting up such parallels.

In *The Audience of Beowulf* Dorothy Whitelock proposes, in a theory generally accepted today, that *Beowulf* was composed by a Christian poet working with pagan materials well after Christianity had become an integral enough part of the culture for a body of Christian themes and allusions to be standard "public property" through the media of sermons, litany and hymns. There is no doubt that the audience was intended to grasp some or all of these allusions; the question is rather how heavily they were meant to weight the poem.

The Controlling Ethos: Christian or Germanic?

Despite a century and a half of scholarship of the poem, there is still disagreement about the ethos that controls it. This is a fundamental disagreement, which when taken to extremes can result in two different versions of *Beowulf*. G. V. Smithers finds the "meaning" of *Beowulf* "already complete within the Germanic heroic ethos" (quoted by Greenfield, *Interpretation,* p. 156), and Margaret Goldsmith, in *The Mode and Meaning of Beowulf* (London: The Athlone Press, 1970), reads the poem as "the first great medieval allegory of human life and death based on the beliefs of the Western Church" (p. viii). To understand a little more clearly the positions represented by these two writers, it is useful to have a definition of allegory. Greenfield says:

> Certainly for Old English literature *allegoria* cuts across formal categories, and we may best enlarge our concept of genre to include this designing spirit. We can refer to it either as a 'non-formal' genre, or, with Mrs. Goldsmith, as a '*mode* of figurative writing' which might inhere only intermittently in a given work. Whatever we call it, allegory, as relevant to the Old English Christian experience, is a message of special moral and/or mystical significance encoded in a seemingly 'otherwise' piece of narrative or description.
>
> (*Interpretation*, p. 135)

In other words, and to put it most simply, Smithers (and others) would see *Beowulf* as meaning what the narrative and description says, while Goldsmith (and others) find in the poem a message which might be quite different from what is said on the surface.

In this section I am going to concentrate primarily on Goldsmith's chapter about Hrothgar's sermon and her ensuing discussion of the dragon's treasure. I shall spend several pages on this, because her book is the most comprehensive and learned treatment of the Christianity in *Beowulf* (and available to the poet) that has yet been written, and because the facility with which she uses her learning might well persuade the reader too naive or hurried to be critical of her argument. Against her Christian allegorical interpretation of the sermon and the treasure I shall set Michael Cherniss's reading of the same passages as demonstrating the essentially Germanic orientation of the poem. To this I shall add some suggestions of my own about the importance of the secular attitude toward treasure in *Beowulf*.

In her preface Goldsmith says that her study began when she "first examined the curiously ambivalent treatment of the treasure hoard in *Beowulf* in the light of Hrothgar's 'sermon'" (p. vii), and the conclusion reached in her years of research is that quoted above, that the poem is an allegory written by a poet well-instructed in Christian beliefs. She says that she discovered that Hrothgar's admonition (which she describes as "unmistakably Christian") "could itself be used as a key to unlock the symbolic meaning of Beowulf's life, involving as it does the right use of kingly power and wealth, which seemed to me to be a central concern of the poet."

She reads the opening lines of the "sermon" (1700–1705a) as simple praise of Beowulf, who has just presented Grendel's head and the ancient sword hilt to the king. Then, reading the word which I have translated "steadily" as "with equanimity," she relates the following phrase—

> Steadily you hold
> your strength with discernment . . .
>   (1705–06)

to Augustine's teaching that "a wise man is one whose reason dominates his lower desires, among

which he includes not only the animal character-
istics of man, but also the love of praise and glory
and powers'' (p. 187). Beowulf's wisdom is in control
of these now—as Heremod's was not when he
''allowed himself to be dominated by violent anger
and greed'' (p. 187). There is a moral to be found
in the contrast between Beowulf now and Heremod
in the past: ''The well-ordered man, in whom reason
is dominant, will turn towards the lasting good, not
to these temporal satisfactions, for this is the *lex
aeterna* written in his heart. Thus,'' she concludes,
''there is a discernible Augustinian pattern of thought
throughout Hrothgar's speech'' (pp. 187–188).

One must understand that this leap to an ''Augustinian pattern of thought'' is not in a vacuum but
has been carefully prepared for by a useful survey
chapter about the writings of the Church Fathers
available in monastic libraries, which provided a
direction for Anglo-Saxon thought about metaphy-
sics and ethics. In arguing a case one naturally cites
those sources which best support it, but if the Bible
is notoriously adaptable to supporting conflicting
views, the writings of the Church Fathers are even
more so, and much of Mrs. Goldsmith's Patristic
quotation seems to be offered as a buttress to her
pre-established convictions rather than as evidence
in a controlled argument which takes alternative
views and possibilities into account. For example,
the ethical pattern of Hrothgar's speech, specifically
the thesis that reason should dominate the passions
so that a man turns away from merely temporal

satisfactions, could be derived from the philosophy of Boethius (not "Christian" in orientation) or even from reason alone as in the Pauline doctrine of the *lex aeterna,* the "eternal law" written in the heart to which Goldsmith refers, quite as well as from the writings of Augustine. This is a good example of the way she forces useful analogies farther than the evidence allows.

It is clear from lines 1722–1724 that the exemplum of Heremod is intended as a moral lesson for Beowulf, who has not yet been tested by having a king's political power over men. "The meaning of that lesson is then made plain by a general example of a proud ruler (1724 ff.)," explains Mrs. Goldsmith (p. 188). The ruler's good fortune is his moral undoing. Yet, like the maxim that "power corrupts," the general doctrine that Hrothgar is preaching is, it seems to me, just good sense: smugness and self-satisfaction naturally blind a man to the weaknesses within himself. This observable fact does not need any *auctoritas* (Biblical or patristic source) to confirm it. We have a "historical" lesson in our own time from which such a conclusion might be drawn, in the mistakes of President Nixon. Certainly such a warning as Hrothgar's is worth giving to any prospective ruler.

But at the core of this general example of the proud ruler comes imagery that is clearly Christian: "From lines 1740 to 1768," says Mrs. Goldsmith, "the poet draws on a number of patristic images for temptation and sin, each of which brings with it a complex of doctrine about the nature of man and his spiritual trials . . . The homiletic material used is the common property of Christian teachers'' (p. 193). This is true, and it has been convincingly argued by Dorothy Whitelock in *The Audience of Beowulf* that some of this imagery would be familiar to an eighth-century aristocratic audience in a Christian court. A Christian teacher, someone trained in the rhetorical practices of the Church, or a monk accustomed to meditate upon such imagery in the cloister, would surely have recognized the "complex of doctrine about the nature of man and his spiritual trials''— or at least some of the associations found by Mrs. Goldsmith in this passage. I am in agreement with that much. But I find it doubtful whether a secular audience would be struck by more than the generally scriptural symbolism of the soul's guardian and the archer adversary of lines 1741b–1747 (which I have illustrated in the translation with a drawing from the *Utrecht Psalter* that brings to life precisely this imagery from Psalm 12). I suspect that the patristic implications of the growth imagery (1741), for example, might well be lost on such an audience.

What seems to me quite as interesting as the question of how much the audience would recognize as the rhetoric of the Christian church is the poet's presentation of Hrothgar as the preacher. As elsewhere, the poet is carefully reticent about how much he allows his protagonist to "know." When Hrothgar gazes upon the sword hilt, on which is written "the long ago beginnings of strife'' (1689), the poet tells us, his audience, what is inscribed there, the fall of the giants (mentioned in Genesis) and the first owner's name, in runes. We are not told that Hrothgar knows about the flood or understands specifically what he sees. Yet even though he cannot be acquainted with scriptural history, which is specific, he is able to make use of scriptural imagery, which is general, having to do with the condition of man. And even though he can have no sense of the reverberations of his own imagery, it is probable that the poet intended his imagery to be understood by the audience in Christian terms, much as Mrs. Goldsmith suggests.

She goes much farther than this, though, when she argues for the relevance to *Beowulf* of a passage in St. Ambrose's *Hexameron* (a discussion of the six days of creation). Ambrose, in his meditation upon the making of Adam, says Goldsmith,

> joins together three of the themes woven into Hrothgar's sermon: arrogance in a time of plenty, the need for a vigilant watch against the Enemy, and the venemous wounds which are caused by the Devil's promptings . . . As Hrothgar goes on to speak of death and man's inevitable parting from his treasured possessions, so Ambrose continues with thoughts of the vanity of earthly treasure, and the ruin of the house, the body itself being but ash . . . The particular combination found in the *Hexameron* suggests not only the outline of Hrothgar's sermon but even the outlook of the whole poem, in which Hrothgar's great hall awaits destruction, Beowulf's hard-won treasure profits no-one, and at the end

the mourners circle the ashes of the hero" (pp. 195–196).

The reader may well feel by this time that the usefulness of Mrs. Goldsmith's methods for our understanding of the poem has passed its limits. But a few more of her points about the "sermon" must be mentioned because they have to do with the fight for the dragon's treasure later.

1. She links the "death-bringer" (or killer, of 1743) and his evil suggestions (1746) with the gaping jaws of Leviathan by way of a passage from the *Moralia* of Gregory the Great.

2. She links the life-as-warfare theme with avarice and temptation, chiefly by way of discussions of Psalm 38:7 (Protestant version Psalm 37) by Gregory and Aldhelm.

3. She says that the mention of the soul's guardian and the killer with his sinister promptings "requires in the speaker [Hrothgar] some belief in the separate existence of soul and body, leading *inescapably* [my italics] to thoughts of life after death." (For one contrasting Old Testament view among many, see Psalm 92, Protestant Psalm 91; our post-revelation understanding of the salvation imagery in this psalm adds meanings about life after death which it did not have for the original Psalmist. Could this not be true also of the similar set of images used by Hrothgar?)

She concludes the chapter on Hrothgar's sermon by saying that by means of the speech "the poet creates an expectation in his hearers that in the second part of the poem they will be shown the contest between an older and more vulnerable Beowulf and the enraged Leviathan, and the hero's meeting with death'' (p. 209).

Though Mrs. Goldsmith's chapter has been tightly written, I do not think I have given an unfair impression of her argument in this critical summary. In my view she has crossed the tenuous line between reading possible interpretations in and reading them into a literary work. In her suggestions of what a homiletically erudite audience might infer from Hrothgar's speech, I think she is on the right track and simply goes too far. But it leads her to go wrong later, which is quite another matter.

Commentators naturally relate Beowulf's account of his virtuous life (2732–43) to Hrothgar's admonition about how a noble life should be lived. Margaret Goldsmith uses this passage as a link between Hrothgar's advice and Beowulf's fight with the dragon. She compares Beowulf's list of evils not done to the short Psalm 14 (Protestant version 15), which a later commentator calls a ''description of noble solders'' because, he explains, the fourth verse, *ad nihilam deductus est . . . malignus,* refers to the Evil One. (The Psalm must be read for the imaginative flight of Goldsmith's conclusion, by way of the above commentator, to be fully appreciated.) ''Thus, the underthought of Psalm 14 has the same tenor as Hrothgar's sermon and concerns the conquest of the Enemy by the just soul,'' she says. ''It seems to me that Beowulf's enumeration of these lesser virtues was meant to call up such thoughts as underlie the description of God's soldier in the psalm, harking back to Hrothgar's admonitory speech and thus bringing the allegorical significance of the dragon fight to the fore" (p. 223).

This is the way she interprets the allegory of the dragon fight:

"The rifling of the hoard, by exhibiting the dragon's costly cup to Beowulf and his men, lets loose the fiery breath of Leviathan through the kingdom. Beowulf suffers unwonted disturbance of mind and a sense of estrangement from God (2329 ff). He is enticed by the thought of treasure and the fame that will accrue to him if he wins it. His challenge to the dragon allegorically represents his attempts to repulse this thought, but he is already spiritually weakened . . . The dragon is quelled, but not before Beowulf has been wounded in the neck by his venomous teeth . . . a wound in the neck—a part of the body often associated with pride —and from this the slow poison spreads through him . . . It is thus reasonable to regard Beowulf as a just man who has fought the good fight during his lifetime, but who is in the end brought to death by the flaws in his human nature, the legacy of Adam's sin, in trying to fight the Dragon alone . . . Through cupidity, Adam and his sons exchanged eternal life for brief possession of earthly goods . . ."
(pp. 235–239)

Before leaving Margaret Goldsmith's discussion,

I think it should be mentioned that her enthusiasm for her theory that Beowulf is driven by cupidity leads her to balance her arguments unfairly. Here are two examples of different ways in which she suppresses what does not support her interpretation. First, in her discussion of Beowulf's giving of his life for worldly treasure like "Adam and his sons," she ignores, or only refers obliquely to, the lines in which he himself tells us why he did this, for his people. Second, in the discussion of the allegorical significance of the dragon's cup (p. 144), she refers to Gregory's statement that gold signifies "the splendour of temporal glory" in a way that implies he takes it as a sign which signifies one thing only, whereas in fact he goes on to say that gold can also signify "the splendour of sanctity"—by which token the cup could then be a sort of grail demanding rescue from the Ancient Enemy who holds it, if one wished to push a contrary interpretation so far! If Mrs. Goldsmith were to say, "Of course Gregory symbolizes gold as both good and evil, but it is the symbolism of evil which is of interest here," her ensuing argument would be more fair.

Nevertheless, after her complex discussions, Michael Cherniss's wholly opposite conclusions in *Ingeld and Christ: Heroic Concepts and Values in Old English Christian Poetry* (The Hague: Mouton, 1972) about the secular nature of Hrothgar's advice seem simplistic:

> "Hrothgar's 'sermon', then, need not be about theological pride and covetousness, even though

pride and covetousness appear there as secular, heroic virtues. Hrothgar concerns himself with the duties and proper conduct of Germanic lords, and with the glory which they may lose if they fail to fulfil the ideals upon which that glory is founded. The speech is not a Christian homily, even though it may contain echoes of the poet's Christian background. Significantly, at the end of the poem Beowulf dies confident that he has followed Hrothgar's advice: he has protected his people from their enemies (2732–2736), has not slain his kinsmen (2739–2743), and has, he believes, won treasure for his followers to enjoy after his death (2794–2798). The description of his funeral confirms the fact that he has won in his lifetime glory which will live after him (3155–3182). Hrothgar's 'sermon' is important, perhaps central to the poem, not because it reveals a Christian view of life, but because it gives expression to secular ideals which control the conduct of Germanic heroes.''

(p. 149)

I do not believe that the Christian and heroic interpretations of Hrothgar's speech need be so mutually exclusive as both Goldsmith and Cherniss suggest. The speech gives expression to those ideals which control conduct within the secular world of the poem (pre-Christian in that the Geats and Danes have not yet been offered the gospel message), while at the same time it reveals the Christian view of the poet and those who are spiritually inclined among his audience; the tone of the poem would suggest that this audience was sympathetic toward those ancestors who lived by the virtues that they knew. While Hrothgar gives appropriate political and spiritual advice to an aspiring young hero who will doubtless come to power, he says more than he knows; what he says in the sixth-century world of the poem will awaken associations for at least some of his later Christian audience, adding meanings for that audience which would be unavailable to Hrothgar himself in his more limited cultural context.

Despite their differences, Goldsmith and Cherniss come to similar conclusions regarding wealth and treasure. Goldsmith finds "the right use of kingly power and wealth" a central concern in the poem, and Cherniss finds "heroic antipathy toward the unrighteous possession of wealth" the key to an understanding of the dragon fight. But whereas Goldsmith's entire focus is upon the inner spiritual meaning of treasure, Cherniss puts the emphasis upon its social meaning:

> In contrast to the thief's secretive approach to the barrow Beowulf, who will prove himself worthy of the hoard, calls the dragon forth to battle in a heroic manner (2550 ff). Beowulf, like Sigemund (884 ff), will earn his treasure, and the honor which it represents, by winning a great martial victory. Beowulf's retainers, with the single exception of Wiglaf, fail to support their lord when he has need of them, and consequently can earn no share in the victory or the hoard. Wiglaf, in his first speech to the retainers (2631–60), emphasizes the gifts which they have already received from their lord, and says that

it is not "fitting" (*gerysne*, 2653) that they should carry shields (which are treasures, and therefore symbolic of the merit of those who bear them) to the place of battle, and then fail to use them in support of their lord . . . After the battle, the retainers return "ashamed" (*scamiende*, 2850) with the shield and arms whose significance their conduct has belied, and they are severely reproached by Wiglaf (2860–91) . . . He predicts evil days to come for the Geats because their symbols of valor no longer have any meaning.

(pp 89–90)

Margaret Goldsmith's remark that some critics have "read into the poem a change from the traditional hero's motives of eagerness for personal glory and gold to an eagerness to serve the people even at the risk of death" (p. 225) suggests that she has little understanding of what treasure meant to the secular Anglo-Saxon aristocrat, a central point made by Hrothgar. It is a material symbol of human worth (or "glory") only so long as it is in use or at the service of the people. There is no question of reading in a change of motive here, because the personal and social values were inextricably related. A king is a gold-friend, a treasure-giver. Even the young "retainer" who mourns for St. Guthlac when he dies calls the saint a *sinc-giefa* "treasure-giver" (*Guthlac*, 1352), though here one assumes that the treasures are of a spiritual nature. As we know from lines 168–169 in *Beowulf*, the gift-throne represents the almost numinous power center of the kingdom, and "that is a good king" who distributes treasures and receives them, as Hrothgar does, from his *gifstol*.

Thus the center of power requires gold to function, and when the dragon has burnt down his hall, Beowulf rightly seeks to renew his kingdom's wealth as well as ridding the Geats of a destructive enemy. This kingly duty does not appear to be what his mind turns to first; his first response seems to be that of a hero, who is not responsible in the same way to his people. Whereas a king's duty is primarily to provide a powerful and charismatic center for his nation, the hero's duty is to put himself at risk to protect this center and win glory for himself and his nation, a glory expressed in songs and portable treasure. A question which many have asked is "how far should Beowulf the king put himself at risk to win a hero's glory?" This question is concerned with cultural values, whereas Margaret Goldsmith's objection to Beowulf's insistence on confronting the dragon alone is that it demonstrates the spiritual pride warned against in Hrothgar's sermon, and results in Beowulf's greed for the gold which was meant for his people (the text certainly does not support this final supposition).

In the earliest critical appraisals of *Beowulf,* scholars thought it was a fine Germanic poem with clumsily interpolated Christian passages. The allegorists tend to offer the flip side of this coin: for Goldsmith, for example, the Christian allegory that she finds in *Beowulf* is opposed to the secular surface of the poem in such a way that it subverts it and becomes superior to it, and the critic's disapproval (disguised as the poet's) falls now upon the pagan Beowulf instead of on the Christian redactor. On the other hand, while those who concentrate upon the cultural level of meaning in *Beowulf* may not appear to contort the poem so radically, I feel that they tend to under-value the importance of the Christian passages.

Scriptural Archetypes as a Solution to the Problem

I do not think that the poet intended to set in opposition the pagan (or secular) and Christian ele-ments in such a way as to diminish the value of either. Instead I believe that he intended to extend the meaning of the secular core of the poem through his use of scriptural archetypes. In the abstract of my article, "The Great Feud: Scriptural History and Strife in *Beowulf*," *PMLA*, 93 (1978), 973–981, I have expressed the thesis as clearly as I could that beneath the fights in *Beowulf* lies the image of a greater fight:

> Dorothy Whitelock describes family and national feuds in *Beowulf* as "sub-plots" to the monster fights. But the theme of feud history is more com-plex than that. There are the Scandinavian fights, some of them perceived and all relevant within the heroic world of the story, and the Great Feud of sacred history, associated in its beginnings with the monster fights in Denmark and in its end with the dragon fight in Geatland. This cosmic feud, intro-duced in the "scripturizing" passages of the poem,

is not perceived within the world of the story. By distinguishing between the kind of knowledge available in that world and the kind available to his audience, the poet foregrounds the theme of the Great Feud and aligns the noble pagans of the poem with God, thereby "redeeming" the cultural identity of an audience for whom the Scandinavian matter of *Beowulf* is ancestral lore.

My view of *Beowulf* is that the poet is not encoding a message allegorically through his work, but rather that he is using allusions to scriptural history to give an added symbolic dimension to secular events. This interpretation is radically different from Margaret Goldsmith's, principally in that the emphasis is seen as not on the message allegorically encoded but on the story itself, with extended significance. For example, in the world of the poem the Danes are beset by monsters; they see these foes "existentially" (as Andreas Haarder has said recently), knowing of no reason for their enmity. We are told, however, that these monsters are descended from Cain, who struck the first blow against a good man and was exiled for his deed. His "family," then, giants and orcs and the like, continue the feud. This information would mean nothing to those in the poem, because they have no knowledge of scriptural history and have not heard of Cain. But for us it offers an illumination about the nature of Grendel's attack, not so "existential" as it seemed, and it aligns him on the side of evil in a feud far greater and with its roots more ancient than those in the poem could perceive. This does not mean that I see the poem as ''about'' the Great Feud, as an allegory. Not at all. Rather I see this element, the scriptural history, as offering us some added information, an extra angle on the events that take place in the poem.

In the end Goldsmith sees Beowulf the hero damned as the result of cupidity, of greed for the treasure. Cherniss sees him as a Germanic hero, no more. I see him as having achieved a hero's glory within the world of the poem, as having won the love of his people to the extent that they burn that great and costly treasure with him, and as having fought worthily, but unaware of the dimensions of his fight, on the side of good in a great scheme of cosmic history.

IV STRUCTURE

Introduction

The impression one receives from a summary of
Beowulf, often strengthened by reading through a
translation quickly, is that, far from being a unified
story of a hero who fights monsters, the poem falls
into two or three parts: the story of a battle against
Grendel, then against his mother, both in Denmark,
and the story of a fight with a dragon in Geatland.
Apart from the person of Beowulf himself there may
seem to be little interrelation or connection between
these narratives. Moreover, frequent digressions are
found in each part; some of these deal with details
of the life of Beowulf, filling out his character and
background, but many appear to have little direct
connection with the narrative. As one becomes more
familiar with the poem and its language, however,
certain sets of themes and images are seen to recur,
complicated identifications and parallels are discovered, and both verbal and symbolic connections
appear to bridge the two parts of the poem, or a
development is seen in the accounts of the three
fights.

Consciousness of a structure in the poem has
emerged over the years in just this way. At first critics

asked only whether *Beowulf* was a unified poem, or conceived as a unity; today most of those who study *Beowulf* as a literary text assume its unity and proceed to trace thematic or stylistic features that bear out their particular theory. There are still those, however, who argue against unity, or complex unity, or who find that the appearance of unity in *Beowulf* is fortuitous.

Three early critics illustrate this divergence of opinion. In a series of articles in 1815–1820 the first critic of *Beowulf,* the Danish scholar Grundtvig, defended the poem as a magnificent attempt to compose a unified story about a hero who fought monsters representative of major evil. He was the only early critic to consider the poem primarily as a work of art, and after wrestling with the problem of its artistry for some time, using the Neoclassical standards of his time, he sadly concluded that the poet failed in what he was trying to do. We may say of Grundtvig what he said of the poet: "The eye saw straight, but the hand erred." The more influential early theories about structure were those proposed by Müllenhoff and Chadwick. In 1889, on the basis of previous Homeric and Biblical scholarship, Müllenhoff evolved his *liedertheorie,* or "theory of lays." He saw the poem as a medley of lays composed by five or six different authors whose work could be distinguished on the basis of their preoccupations. The last redactor, according to Müllenhoff, marred his original by putting in his preoccupations with Christian morality. In 1926 Professor Chadwick described the poem as a native development which told a disjointed narrative story. He saw it as little more than an entertainment for a long winter's night.

Views analogous to these three continue to be expressed in more contemporary theories about the poem's structure, though since Tolkien's lecture of 1936 those who have perceived in *Beowulf* some kind of thematic unity binding the parts together far outnumber those who have not.

The Poem as a Unity

Professor Tolkien describes *Beowulf* as a heroic elegy, not an epic: the figure of one man is the unifying plot device, while the unifying tone of the poem is elegaic. The poem is successfully organized in two parts which comprise the rise and fall of a hero who faces monsters symbolic of evil (here he unknowingly echoes Grundtvig's earlier view). Much of Tolkien's argument is a refutation of an earlier claim that the poet failed as an artist because he put the irrelevant mythological monsters in the center of his poem and relegated the important "epic" matters concerning the rise and fall of nations to the circumference. In Tolkien's opinion the poet is concerned with something more widely significant than the political scene of early Scandinavia. His subject is the condition of the individual in the world and in society: "Beowulf is a man, and for him and many that is tragedy enough." In the end, after many successes, he, like Thor (and like each of us), must engage in the inevitable last battle against overwhelming odds. Despite the fact that it is impossible to remain unmoved by Tolkien's eloquence, even stripped of the rhetoric his claims for unity remain reasonable, based on what is in the poem.

In rejecting the major symbolic significance of the monster fights and in returning to the theory that *Beowulf* is an epic about the fall of nations, Tolkien's two most important followers, Bonjour and Brodeur, are less successful in arguing for the overall unity of the poem. This is partly because both are primarily concerned with analyzing smaller sections of *Beowulf* in order to demonstrate the conscious artistry of the poet.

Bonjour, in *The Digressions in Beowulf* (1950), sets out to analyze how the various digressions add to their context and to the structure of the whole. Sometimes he loads his argument unfairly in favor of the poet; although he says he will remain objective in giving evidence to support his views, he patently does not. Whatever strictures one might place on his handling of individual examples, however, the weight of his evidence is on the whole convincing, that these at first sight unrelated passages add to the thrust of the poem. He distinguishes between episodes and digressions by describing an episode as merged into the main narrative, like the Breca episode, while a digression is an actual break from the narrative, like the Sigemund story. A list of the principle episodes and digressions follows this section, as a useful aid in reading the poem.

Bonjour's analysis of the artistic function of the section on Shield (an episode) is a good example of his method. In the first half of the poem the function of the Shield episode is to imply the parallel between Shield and Beowulf (both saviors of the Danes), to set up Beowulf as a hero by contrast with the greatness of the Danes, to introduce the Heremod motif, and to establish the setting of a great court (one could almost say the passage gives us the genealogy of Heorot). Furthermore, the episode anticipates the motif of "leaderless time" so important in the second half of the poem, and strikes a perfect balance with the evocative funeral scenes at the end.

According to Bonjour, the digressions function as unifying factors in three main ways: they add a lively background to the poem; they keep the audience in touch with real historical events (what, in Bonjour's opinion, the poem is in some sense "really about"); and they introduce emotional and thematic undercurrents which give the poem added dimensions. Bonjour shares Tolkien's view of the general "rising and falling" structure of the poem, but says that *Beowulf* is an epic representing the fall of the Geatish nation.

Brodeur, in *The Art of Beowulf* (1959), also sees the poem as a two-part structure, with each part ending with a summary of the character of the hero. At the end of part one is Hrothgar's homily on the ideal champion and retainer, and at the end of part two are the elegies for the ideal king. The poem relates the tragedy of a noble hero who fails to save his people, through conquests that succeed on a primary level: though Grendel is slain Heorot falls; though the dragon is slain the Geats fall. Again this is a standard epic theme.

Brodeur is most successful in his critical appreciation of particular passages, showing that in these the poet is a conscious and highly original artist (especially in Chapter IV, "Design for Terror"). His main argument for unity, however, seems to be that if the poet is good in creating individual episodes, he must be good in designing overall structure. He perhaps goes farthest astray in suggesting that Beowulf's devotion to Hygelac is the unifying theme of the poem, though it is perfectly true that the thane/king relationship gives Beowulf much of his character.

Robert E. Kaske, in "*Sapientia et Fortitudo* as the Controlling Theme of *Beowulf*," *Studies in Philology*, 55 (1958), 423–57 (reprinted in the Nicholson anthology), puts forward an argument of quite a different kind. Kaske believes that the Old Testament concept of wisdom and bravery as heroic ideals controls the action, and that beneath the heroic garb of the story the poem is ecclesiastically oriented (he makes a better case for this than most of the scholars who use the methods of medieval exegesis in interpreting the poem). He sees the poem as a three-part structure, corresponding to the three fights, through which Beowulf progresses from ideal warrior *(fortitudo)* to ideal king *(sapientia)*.

These critics all see the poem as composed of two parts that balance or three parts that progress. Others have found a non-linear unity in the poem. The most extreme of these, Thomas Hart, wrote a dissertation on his theory that *Beowulf* is structured like various other medieval and Latin works on a balanced system of numbers; he found various complex schemes, but the basic one is 33 fits (counting the Shield prelude as one) containing 7 x 330 + 1 (= 2311) lines, followed by 11 fits containing 3 x 290 + 1 (= 871) lines. John Leyerle's theory is more attractive. In his article, "The Interlace Structure of *Beowulf*," *University of Toronto Quarterly*, 37 (1967), 1–17, he proposes that themes in the poem interlace like the delicate zoomorphic spirals in Anglo-Saxon art, and like the *entrelacement* of later French romances; he finds a contemporary literary source that to some degree supports his thesis. His theory has on the whole been more influential in the analysis of themes than of overall structure. The most useful analysis so far, for me at least, is John D. Niles' "Ring Composition and the Structure of *Beowulf*," *PMLA* 94 (1979), 924–935, from which I have reproduced the diagram at the beginning of this book.

The Poem as an Oral Aggregation

The more extreme Oral Formulaicists, those who believe that *Beowulf* was an extemporaneous oral composition based on a highly traditional and skilled command of oral formulas, would reject the arguments for conscious artistry in the poet's use of recurrent themes and—in particular—of recurrent phrases that appear to hold the poem together. They would reject this evidence on the grounds that the poet's vocabulary and even his stock of ideas was limited by his inherited form, hence the repetitions. In a sense a return to Müllenhoff's idea that the poem is a series of traditional elements strung together over a long period, this theory is far more sophisticated: though the language is mainly a series of traditional formulas and the plot of the poem has developed by aggregation, handed down from one singer to another, the final result is fairly organic. But the appearance of any specifically literary consciousness on the part of a single poet who conceived his work as a unity is both fortuitous and a contradiction in terms, as the poem was an oral "folk" composition. As recent studies have shown that even those Old English poets who derive their subjects from obvious Latin models work within the formulaic tradition, this theory has been much modified.

The Poem as Unstructured

Sisam, in *The Structure of Beowulf* (1965), attacks the Bonjour and Brodeur school. Although he commends the poet's artistry in creating the "mood of the moment," he shows that many of the now accepted views upon which theories about the poem's structure have been based are assumptions rather than facts. Some of the things he argues against in his short book are Tolkien's idea of a rising and falling structure with the unifying theme of a symbolic fight-against-doom; the value of the Heremod /

Sigemund digression as contrast and parallel to Beowulf; the dense interrelationship of Wealtheow and
Hildeburh with the irony that this supposes about
Hrothulf's position in Heorot; and the long-standing
idea that Beowulf's death marked the collapse of
the Geatish nation (and the subsequent establishment of the Kingdom of Sweden). He suggests that
too often the plain meaning of the poem is overlooked in favor of dark hints, and says that while
he is not hostile to conjectures, they should not be
the basis for larger arguments. He describes *Beowulf*
as a heroic narrative meant primarily to entertain a
possibly illiterate audience of Anglo-Saxons, and asks
what was their response, what could they respond to?
Measuring *Beowulf* by classical standards of structure,
he concludes, is unfair to a poem great in its own
right.

Though his criticism is destructive and not always
convincing, Sisam's book is important. Tolkien
awakened the first broad interest in this aspect of the
poem, and Sisam is voicing the opinion of many
that those who appreciate the poet's subtlety are
often prone to read into the poem what is not there.
He does not take into account, however, many of
the subtleties that are there.

Summary

The arguments for the artistic structure of *Beowulf*
tend to be based upon a theory that the poem contains a central theme or meaning, a "moral" that
unifies the poem, which the poet conveyed with
more or less success (even Leyerle, who does not need

81

to, finds a meaning in his pattern). This urge to find such a centrifugal force has led to many misreadings or over-readings of the text (especially when an allegorical interpretation has been at stake). The less successful argument for unity in *Beowulf,* that it is essentially an epic, puts the importance on things that the poet himself does not place at the center of his poem. The arguments that any unity is fortuitous and that the question of overall structure is irrelevant are usually based on the proposition that there was no single poet and that *Beowulf* was not conceived as a written poem, while the arguments that *Beowulf* has no structure rest primarily on the premise that no single moral or epic intention was in the poet's mind. It is my own opinion that the poet's intention to compose the poem as a unified whole seems clear from his use of identification, motifs, and digressions to build up a scheme of increasing allusiveness and balance from one part of the poem to another, so that "the exposition of his fable" (to use Francis Bacon's words) "doth fall out with great felicity."

Today when people speak of the structure of *Beowulf,* they usually refer tacitly to one of two models. The first is more truly literary: a linear model, moving through time. Those who discuss "the meaning" of the poem often think of *Beowulf* in terms of this model. The second model is borrowed from art: a static design. Those concerned with themes often see *Beowulf* this way. The poem is sufficiently complex to provide evidence for either model.

Digressions and Episodes: A List

Lines

Song as a Special Kind of Digression, and the Finnsburg Story

When the *Beowulf* poet tells us that the *shope* sings a tale appropriate to an occasion, he does not then give us that story verbatim as it is heard in Heorot. Instead he paraphrases it or meditates upon it, giving us something quite different, related to the theme of the *shope*'s song but organized in a way that furthers his own tale. Thus the creation song in Heorot celebrates not only the building of that great hall but the beginning of the story itself, and it introduces the demon Grendel even as it evokes him. As I have pointed out in the notes, that song, after it ends for the audience in Heorot, continues on into scriptural history for the Beowulf poet's audience, thus setting the events in Heorot into a larger "cosmic" perspective. Likewise the story of

Sigemund is not what the *shope* sang but an epitome, introducing the dragon theme that the poet will develop later. I believe that when the poet digresses on the subject of Hama and the Brosinga *mene*, the *shope* is again singing a song behind the digression; this is an unorthodox view. While he sings, the poet digresses even farther to tell us the fate of the golden collar that Beowulf is receiving.

But by far the longest section of material in *Beowulf* that does not pertain immediately to the story is the section commonly called the "Finnsburg episode." Again, as the poet tells us his version of the story of Finnsburg, he moves right away from the tale of courage that the *shope* must have sung to celebrate Beowulf's heroic deed. Instead of a battle lay, the poet tells us of the terrible results of battle, of a woman's sorrow as her son and her brother lie dead, and of a man trapped by conflicting vows and a need for vengeance. The episode as told by the poet sets the stage for Wealtheow's concern about her own two sons, and for the sorrowful vengeance of Grendel's mother. But this is the poet's own meditation upon the emotional agonies surrounding a well-known heroic event; it is not the tale that the *shope* sings in Heorot.

The following fragment of a lay, copied down by the antiquarian Hickes from a manuscript that was later lost, gives us some idea of the nature of the song about Finnsburg that the *shope* might actually have sung. It is true Anglo-Saxon battle poetry. A comparison of this vivid fragment with the slower paced and thoughtful episode in *Beowulf* tells us much about the *Beowulf* poet's methods as he drew upon traditional materials well known to his audience. My translation here is based both on Klaeber's text and that of Donald K. Fry, *Finnsburg: Fragment and Episode* (London: Methuen and Co., Ltd., 1974). Fry discusses the many problems of text and interpretation in his introduction to this volume.

Since in the fragment the Danish leader Hnaef is still alive, whereas the episode in *Beowulf* opens with the scene of Hildeburh mourning for him and her son, the fragment must precede the episode in the order of events. The battle begins at night, with the moon flicking in and out among the clouds. The two contending forces are the visiting Danes, in the guest hall, and the native Frisians, outside. The fragmentary opening is usually thought to be a question asked by one of the Danes when he sees a flash in the outer darkness, but as the punctuation is editorial, it is also possible to read it as part of a statement.

                         "... Horns aflame?"

Then Hnaef began chanting, young chieftain
    in war:
"No dawn is this rising, nor a dragon flying,
nor is it the horns of this hall aflame.

5   It is them, bearing arms at us! Birds cry out,
    the wild wolf howls, the war-spear roars,
    shield answers shaft! Now shines this moon,
    wandering in the clouds. Now deeds of woe
    rise to perform the strife of this folk.

10   Therefore, awake now, warriors mine!
      Hold high your shields, think hard of courage,
      turn to the battle, bear yourselves bravely!''

      Gold-armored they rose then, girding on
          weapons.
      To one door strode the splendid warriors
15   Sigeferth and Eaha, swinging their swords,
      and to the other went Ordlaf and Guthlaf,
      and Hengest himself came hard on their tracks.

      Outside, Guthere was pleading with Garulf
      not to fight in that first attack
20   or flaunt his armor before those doors,
      for fierce was the warrior who wished to take it.
      But high and clear, keen young Garulf
      hurled his question: who held those doors?

      ''My name is Sigeferth,'' said he, ''of the
          Sedgas,
25   a prince well known for experienced warfare.
      For you, the outcome is already certain,
      which fate you will choose, if you challenge
          me!''

      Then a roar of slaughter arose in that building.
      Shields held high by the warriors were
          shattered,
30   heads burst open, the hall-floor thundered,
      until at that fight Garulf fell,
      the first of those dwelling in Finn's land,
      Guthlaf's son, and good men around him
      sank as corpses where the raven circled

35   swarthy and gleaming. Sword-light flashed
as though all Finnsburg were on fire!

Never have I heard of warriors more worthy,
of sixty who bore themselves better in battle
or gave more return for the shining mead,

40   than those young heroes did to Hnaef.
They fought five days, and not a man fell
of that hardy band, and they held the doors.
At last, wounded, a warrior lay dying.
He said that his battle-shirt had been broken,

45   that hardest of byrnies, and his helmet
       pierced, too.
Then at once the leader of those warriors asked
how others were bearing up under their
       wounds,
or which of the young men . . .

(Later in the fight Hnaef himself is slain. His
place as leader of the Danish party is taken
by Hengest, who eventually must agree to a
truce with the Frisians when neither side has
the force to continue fighting.)

Addendum: Women in *Beowulf,*
an Argument for Tripartite Structure

The next time a guide to *Beowulf* is written, such a section as this will be integrated into the text. The fact that in this case it is an addendum shows how long ago the book first took shape (as a course for Wolsey Hall, Oxford, in the sixties—it is with the blessings of their vice-principal and director of courses that it appears as a book at all). As I write now in 1986 there are three recent books on Anglo-Saxon women that change or modify our understanding of their importance in society and literature: Helen Damico's learned comparative study of *Beowulf's Wealhtheow and the Valkyrie Tradition* (1984), in which her aim is "to give Wealhtheow's character literary moorings, and . . . a legendary base" (p. 180), Christine Fell's more general and historical survey of *Women in Anglo-Saxon England* (1984), and Jane Chance's analysis of specifically literary modes in *Woman as Hero in Old English Literature* (1986), where she particularly draws a distinction in the way the passive peacemaker and the active woman leader (or hero) are regarded, with the latter "good" only if she is chaste and "Christian," or at least identifiable with the Virgin Mary as opposed to wicked Eve who usurps the male role of political decision-maker. There has also been a series of articles and papers clarifying our understanding of the role of women in the culture and the literature of the period, among which Alexandra Hennesey Olsen's chapter on "Women in *Beowulf*," in *Approaches to Teaching Beowulf,* edited by Jess B. Bessinger, Jr., and Robert F. Yeager for The Modern Language Association of America (1984), should especially be consulted as providing an excellent overview. It is obvious that the topic has come of age in the past few years.

I draw attention to these works in this chapter because the importance we assign to the role of women in the poem affects our understanding of its structure. In Tolkien's vision of the rising-falling structure emphasizing youth and age, Beowulf's fights with Grendel and the Dragon receive the focus so that the fight with Grendel's mother becomes structurally negligible, an appendage (like this section). But by reading *Beowulf* as a tripartite poem, this middle section, in which the concern of mothers about their sons is a central motif, receives its appropriate weight (see Olsen, p. 151).

I believe that it is symptomatic of written scholarship in general, or has been until now, that while I have always made a point of the contrast between Wealtheow and Grendel's mother in my teaching, and stressed how Wealtheow's response to the Finnsburg story is in terms of her own situation (as I have mentioned above on p. 84), I neglected these important matters in the notes to my translation. Niles' diagram of the structure of *Beowulf* at the beginning of this book may serve as a corrective as it emphasizes the importance of the central woman-focused section in a particularly interesting way; structurally, the poem becomes a palindrome, with each matching "side" focused inward upon Beowulf's descent into the mere to confront Grendel's enormous mother. This is where myth transcends ethnicity to offer suggestive evidence pertinent to a number of contemporary concerns—as does the very need to revise our concept of the structure itself.

V STYLE

The difficult passages in *Beowulf,* and such important questons as how the poet really felt about his
hero and the heroic ethic (did he condemn it in the
end?), give rise to much disagreement about the
poem, but few who read it in Old English under normal circumstances (that is, not under compulsion
and not hedged about with dated critical standards
having nothing to do with the poem) will disagree
about the general impact of the style. The overall
style of *Beowulf* has been described as "grand,"
"epic" (referring to amplitude), and "compelling."

The best way to get a sense of this aspect of the
style, even in a translation, is to read the poem like
any narrative, quickly in the what-happened-next
passages and more reflectively in the poet's asides,
but aloud, and with projection if possible, remem-
bering that whatever the precise nature of the audience (cloistered or secular) *Beowulf* was very probably composed for oral delivery in a high and resonant
wooden hall filled with friendly kinspeople. A sense
of the audience is part of a sense of this poem: it is
an assured poem, flung out with the certainty that it
will be well received. But like Shakespeare's plays,
representing oral poetry of another kind, *Beowulf*
also lends itself to examination of the smaller details

of style. This section of the Guide will list and describe some of the particular rhetorical effects in *Beowulf* which contribute to the richness and nuances of the poem.

Alliteration and Rhythm

Old English poetry is distinguished by a four-beat line bound together by "beginning rhyme" or alliteration, a similar sound at the beginnings of stressed syllables rather than at the ends of words. I have imitated this form in my translation:

4   Often Shield Shefing shattered the courage
       of troops of marauders by taking their mead-
           seats.

In the first of these two lines the alliteration is on *sh*, and in the second it is on *t*. (It is not on *m*: the *m* in marauders is not in a stressed syllable. In line 295 *marauders* alliterates with *rests*.)
Alliteration may fall on vowels as well as on consonants in Old English poetry. Here it falls on *e*:

     (Grendel ruled)
145 alone and evil, until empty stood
      the best of houses . . .

Moreover, any stressed vowel-sound may alliterate with any other, as in these lines about Grendel's magical resistance to swords:

801   None of the greatest
       iron blades over all the earth,
       not any sword at all, could ever touch him.

Above all, it must be remembered that this is oral poetry, not a game with letters; it is the sounds that must match:

2233 Once, long ago, a noble warrior . . .

As some of these examples show, only two of the four beats in the line need alliterate. The Old English rule is that the third beat of the line always marks the alliteration, which falls also on the first or second beat or both, never on the fourth. (I found it impossible to follow this rule rigidly in my translation, and frequently alliterate on the fourth beat.)

In addition to binding and marking off the Old English verse-line (as the beat alone could not), alliteration has the function of stressing important words in a sentence. The critic Stanley B. Greenfield argues that the poet sometimes takes advantage of this feature of alliteration to make "a semantic linking via the metrical pattern despite an absence of syntactical dependency." In other words, he may "illogically" link or contrast apparently distinct subjects or ideas across a break between sentences, as in this example:

178   Such was their wont,
       the hope of the heathens; in their hearts they

> thought of
> hell below. They knew not the Lord . . .

In this passage, explains Greenfield (*Critical History*, p. 76), "the hope of the heathens is equated through alliteration and stress with hell," across the sentence break between them. (In the Old English the words "heathen," "hope," and "hell" are in direct sequence in line 179; nevertheless this effect is not wholly lost in the translation.)

The Poet's Word-Hoard

When Beowulf comes to the land of the Danes and is challenged by their sentinel to tell who he is, he "unlocks his hoard of words" (259). This phrase refers to formal speech, as though it were a collection of jewels to be kept in a coffer under lock and key, and taken out for special occasions. The poet, of course, has a word-hoard as rich as a prince's, containing his own special diction and turns of speech.

The words the *Beowulf*-poet uses are often very special. "A large proportion" of the words in the poem, says Klaeber, "is virtually limited to poetic diction," that is, to words not found in Old English prose, of which far more is extant than the poetry. "A good many terms are nowhere recorded outside of *Beowulf*," Klaeber continues, "and not a few of these may be confidently set down as of the poet's own coinage" (p. lxiii). Moreover, the poet uses multitudes of synonyms, especially for kings and retainers, war and weapons, sea and seafaring; his word-hoard is far more ample than ours in these matters of a warrior-society, just as an Eskimo, whose life is closely related to his arctic environment, has many more words for snow than we do. Unfortunately this aspect of the poet's style must be lost in translation. *So sad! But language morphs*

Metaphorical language need not always be lost, and similes are usually easy to retain. Beowulf's "unlocking his hoard of words" (259) is a good example of metaphor, in which one object or action is seen in terms of another with which it bears some resemblance (as in, "my love is a rose"). While metaphorical language is frequent in the poem, simile ("my love is *like* a rose") is rarer and dramatic: when Grendel penetrates Heorot and strides from the shadowy darkness outside onto the floor of the even darker hall, he stares at the sleeping warriors, and from his eyes pours "a horrible light like a flame" (727). One entire digression, "The Father's Lament" (2444–2462) is itself a simile (in this case called an "epic" simile because Homer often uses such long comparisons); here Beowulf is saying that the helplessness Hrethel felt at the accidental slaying of his son is *like* that of a man watching his son being hanged for some crime, unable to avenge him.

"Kennings" are a special kind of condensed metaphor found in Old English and Old Norse poetry. There is one in the tenth line of the poem, "whale's road" for "sea," and they occur throughout, "battle-flame" for "sword," "heath-stepper" for "hart,"

and so forth. Often, because the kenning by its
nature is very close to riddle and I did not wish to
stop the momentum of the poem, I have found it
best to spell these out. But I have tried to retain with
all their force certain kennings which seem to me of
special thematic importance, such as "bone-house"
(3147), which refers to Beowulf's body on the flaming pyre, but also is a metaphor that picks up the
theme of the burning halls of kings throughout the
poem.

Kennings and the more formal riddles that abound
in Old Norse and Old English poetry indicate a particular turn of mind and a culture that delights in
exploring the potentialities of meaning in language.
Perhaps because punning is popularly thought to be
vulgar or trivial, word-play has only recently been
recognized as a significant feature in Old English
poetry. The ancients did not feel it to be vulgar;
quite otherwise. Like Joyce and Hopkins (and some
modern psychologists), they felt that echoes of language revealed truths that were otherwise hidden.

The great example of this is the famous sequence
of puns attributed to Gregory the Great when he saw
a group of fair-haired slave boys in the Roman mar-
ketplace. Upon finding out that they were Angles,
followers of the king Ælla, and from the province of
Deira in North-East England, Gregory said that they
should therefore be the companions of angels, sing
Ælle-luia, and be saved from the wrath *(de ira)* of
God. As I explained some years ago, "The process
of reasoning behind the three puns is based on

Gregory's assumption that verbal similarities tell us something about the essential nature of the thing named. . . . The fact that [the Angles] are heathen and the fact that they are angelic are both 'true' facts simultaneously, though they are contradictory facts. So long as they remain heathen, the pun contains a paradox; by their conversion the temporal paradox will be resolved with the realization of the eternal promise inherent in their names" (quoted by Greenfield, *Interpretation,* p. 85).

Unfortunately, puns based on similar sounds must by their nature be lost in translation from one language to another (unless, like Gregory's punning, they are based on sound-play between languages). I shall comment here only on two rather simple "onomastic" puns (puns based on names). The note on line 874 mentions the word-play in the Old English that introduces the hero Sigemund, whose tale is sung in honor of Beowulf's fight with Grendel. His name, translated "victory hand," makes an appropriate epithet for Beowulf himself, who has just achieved victory with his mighty grip. Later in the poem, Unferth is sitting at the feet of his lords Hrothgar and Hrothulf, who trust his *ferhþe* (which I translate "courage"), "though to his kinsmen / he had done little service at the play of swords" (1167–68). It seems to me that in these lines the poet himself points out the irony of trusting Unferth's *ferhþe*. It does not matter whether or not the word is etymologically related to Unferth's name; the poet is playing with the similar sounds in these words to make a non-logical point, to reinforce an unfortunate aspect of Unferth's character.

Oral formulas, phrases which were to the poet's jewelled words like necklaces or rings into which these jewels could be set, were an important treasure in the poet's word-hoard. Sometimes oral formulas appear in the poems as exact repetitions, but more often they are formulaic phrases into which the relevant word may be set, like the often occurring "X spoke, the son of X," or "That was a sad woman!" (line 1075) and "That was a good king!" (line 2390).

Not many years ago it was thought by some scholars that frequently repeated formulaic phrases, since they occur with variations throughout all Old English poetry, controlled the poet even more than he was capable of controlling them. Sometimes, indeed, they are used unimaginatively, but the *Beowulf* poet is clearly able to manipulate his formulas to achieve his stylistic purposes. Greenfield gives a fine example of the poet's artistry in his use of the "beasts of battle" theme, a formula ("the eagle screams, the wolf howls") which often accompanies accounts of battle and which indeed opens the "Finnsburg Fragment." In *Beowulf* the poet "hoards" this formula, says Greenfield, "not using it in the traditional way in scenes describing the battles against either demons or hostile armies, but reserving it uniquely and climactically for the end of the Messenger's great speech prophesying doom to all of the dead Beowulf's people" (*Critical History,* p. 74).

Stylistic Patterns

Some of the poet's patterns are evident at many levels in the poem. Perhaps the most obvious of these is contrast. Tolkien found a similarity between the "rising and falling" contrastive structure of the Old English poetic line, which typically breaks in the middle, and the structure of the whole of *Beowulf,* which he saw as a "rising" action in the first part of the poem, and a "falling" action in the second (*"Beowulf:* The Monsters and the Critics"). For Greenfield also

> contrasts (and parallels) are what bind the poem into a unity, operating in the larger structural elements, character presentations, theme, and even in the most detailed stylistic matters.
>
> (*Critical History,* pp. 85–86)

The main pattern of contrast he sees is youth vs age, and connected with this theme, the ideal of the perfect retainer in part I and of the perfect king in part II. "The youth-age structural contrast is also related to success and failure, and, in a widening sense, to the rise and fall of nations" (p. 86). Finally, he finds a contrast in tone between the two parts of the poem, heroic in the first part and elegaic in the second.

Certainly patterns of contrast permeate *Beowulf.* Grendel, the "angry" demon, preyed upon the lordly ones who "lived in delight and happy ease" (86–100). Beowulf became a help to his comrades, but hatred took hold of Heremod (914–915). Grendel, the "shadow-walker" (702) moved "under the masses of cloud . . . until he could glimpse the gleams of gold" that marked Hrothgar's hall (714 716). One also finds such contrasts within the line itself, like the alliteratively marked "hope" vs "hell" of line 179 pointed out above.

The "envelope pattern" also may be seen at a structural level and in smaller units. In *The Larger Rhetorical Patterns in Anglo-Saxon Poetry* (New York: Columbia University Press, 1935), Adeline Courtney Bartlett defines the envelope pattern as "any logically unified group of verses bound together by the repetition at the end of (1) words or (2) ideas or (3) words and ideas which are employed at the beginning" (p. 9). The story itself is bracketed between descriptions of funerals. The Sigemund-Heremod digression (867–915) is contained between references to horse-racing. The description of the giants' golden sword-hilt is contained between two statements that Hrothgar "spoke." This pattern occurs at the syntactical level as well.

Understatement and negative construction are two related patterns that describe in terms of what is not. Though the poet sometimes heightens descriptions by the use of superlatives ("the best of houses" at 285, "the greatest torque I have ever heard tell of" at 1196), a more notable figure is his use of *litotes,* or understatement, to achieve a kind of emphasis by negation: "Death is not easy / to hide away from, try it who will!" (1002–03), that is, death is impossible to escape. Edward B. Irving, Jr., devotes nearly a chapter of his book, *A Reading of Beowulf,* to the use of negative constructions, "a striking feature of Germanic rhetoric" in the poem. For example, both by the use of these devices and through contrasting examples of "non-heroes" Beowulf is characterized to a great degree by the things he is not: niggardly of gold, a killer of his kinsmen, bad-tempered, an oath-breaker, and so on.

"The very soul of the Old English poetic style," says Klaeber, is that pattern which today we call "variation." Brodeur's definition is perhaps the simplest we have. He describes strict variation as "a double or multiple statement of the same concept or idea in different words, with a more or less perceptible shift in stress" *(The Art of Beowulf,* p. 40). The most obvious example of variation is the formula "X spoke, the son of X." This is used more artfully when the second phrase is geared to the context. When Grendel's mother has appeared unexpectedly to prey upon the Danes, and Hrothgar must turn once again to Beowulf for help to save his people, the poet does not simply say, as he usually does, "Hrothgar spoke, the lord of the Shieldings," but "Hrothgar spoke, the Shieldings' protector" (1321). Such a parenthetical clarification of the noun (Hrothgar, the Shieldings' protector, spoke) is called apposition. Fred C. Robinson, who is the expert on variation in Old English poetry, says, "I regard variation as apposition . . . if apposition be extended to include restatements of adjectives, verbs, and phrases as well as of nouns and pronouns."

In his chapter on variation in *Old English Poetry: Essays on Style,* edited by Daniel G. Calder, Robinson adds to the above definition a list of the major stylistic functions of variation: "A cluster of variations can prolong dramatically a crucial moment in a poem. A single variation can effect a swift rhetorical transition . . . Variations can register subtle shifts in perspective . . . Variation can introduce rhetorical suspense into a sentence through its effect of artful retardation. And in the best poetry it achieves these effects while simultaneously and effortlessly fulfilling the metrical and alliterative requirements of the verse form."

I shall offer only a few examples. The triple variation on Grendel's approach to Heorot prolongs that crucial moment, shifts the perspective, and introduces suspense:

> In the night he came,
the shadow walker! . . .

> From the moor there came, under misty cliffs,
Grendel striding: he bore God's wrath . . .

> To the hall he came, huge and striding,
doomed, without joy. At once the door
sprang from its hinges . . .

> (702-721)

In each variation of "Grendel coming" he is more concrete—and closer! And, as others have observed, the sonorous repetition of his coming tolls like a bell. A similar narrowing of focus occurs in the following passage:

> To all the Danes it was hard to endure,
> a difficult thing for many a thane,
> for each of those friends, when on the edge
> of that stony cliff they came upon it—
> Ashere's head.
>
> (1418–22)

To come upon the head of an anonymous stranger would be one thing, but these men came upon that of a countryman, their own lord, their friend! Moreover, the variation retards the subject of the sentence, delaying the revelation of the subject, *what* was hard for those Danes to endure, for five lines. We see the words, which slightly lessens the effect; it would have much greater dramatic impact in a poem we only heard.

Such a deliberate retardation of the action to make the climax more spectacular when it arrives also occurs in the following lines, but here the object of the suspense is presented in quite a different way from the above. Here it is an unexpected variation in a list of helps to the hero:

> Edgetheow's son would have ended his days
> there under the pool, the prince would have perished,
> except he was helped by his woven sark,
> that hard net of war—and by holy God . . .
>
> (1550–53)

While in the first two examples above the dramatic perspective shifts and focuses within the action, within the scene in the poem, here it shifts dramatically to right outside the action, to the omniscient point-of-view which the poet so subtly attunes to our own.

Many of these rhetorical patterns in the poem are aided or even made possible by the presence of run-on lines, by the fact that a phrase or sentence need not come to a halt at the end of a line, but can flow smoothly into the next. "*Beowulf* may serve to illustrate the middle stage of the run-on style," writes Kemp Malone in "Plurilinear Units in Old English Poetry," *Review of English Studies,* 19 (1943), 202–03. "Here some of the plurilinear units are of great length; their length may be so great, indeed, that they no longer can be felt as units and include diverse matters." Editors obscure the true flow of these lines by modern English punctuation, and so do I in my translation by trying to make briefer, more comprehensible sentences from the free-flowing materials of this oral poem. In Beowulf's long reminiscence before his last battle, for example, his account of Hrethel's sorrow flows smoothly (more smoothly than my translation shows) into the evocative scene of the hanged boy (2434–2449), in a single sentence.

The Conscious Artistry of the Poet

Once it was thought that many of the *Beowulf* poet's stylistic effects were fortuitous. Klaeber said of the poem that "looseness is, in fact, one of its marked peculiarities," and the critic Gilbert Highet (in a judgment based on long out-of-date assumptions) condemned it more recently as "artistically inferior." But Old English poetry, as I hope even this brief survey of stylistic effects in *Beowulf* shows, has its own formal laws, and they differ, sometimes radically, from those of other poetry with which we might be more familiar.

Today we are beginning to recognize the reasons for some of the poet's methods of which Klaeber complained, such as the "lack of steady advance" in the action, and the "rambling, dilatory method" of presenting events out of sequence. We are beginning to recognize these "faults" as conscious stylistic techniques which are meant to achieve particular results, and which are not at all fortuitous. The first of these two "faults," for example, may be explained as the result of the poet's greater emphasis on the motivations and feelings of his characters than on plot, and on pattern of events than on action narrative. This results in a multiplicity of points of view which more than compensates for the "lack of steady advance." The second "fault" gives us the interlacing of themes which is coming now to be valued as highly artistic.

It also gives us an extra-temporal view of events, a sort of God's-eye view in which past and future events of human history coalesce with present action: the human history of the particular event is set within the larger and more general framework of moral or divine history, symbolized by the recurring "types" or "shadows" of feuding nations and supernatural beings—human history impinging upon a divine conflict between good and evil, with Beowulf, the noble human warrior, at the center. This multiple vision is achieved through various methods and on different levels of subtlety, sometimes by means of a digression, an analogy, or a scriptural allusion, at other times by means of such non-logical stylistic devices as the alliterative binding and the syntactical juxtaposition of elements pointed out by Greenfield. Consider lines 81–83:

> The building towered
> high and wide-gabled—awaiting the hostile
> leap of flames.

From the very moment in time (and line in the poem) that the building of Heorot was completed, that it (in a more exact translation) "*h*eaved up, *h*igh and *h*orn-wide," its fate was inextricably bound up with those "*h*ostile flames" in its future.

A major problem facing early critics of *Beowulf* was that they could not understand this aspect of the poet's vision. They were caught up in the principle that a good story should have "a beginning, a middle, and an end," and should proceed at a regular pace from one stage to another. This is a linear vision, and indeed, story-telling is a linear form, unfolding in time much as the written word proceeds from left to right across the page. As I have worked with Anglo-Saxon poetry, however, I have found in several of the greatest poems, including *Beowulf*, a duality of vision that can best be described as an "expanded consciousness.'' There is the linear story at one level, but embracing that story (or, in other poems, embracing the dramatic situation), there is a consciousness that does not view what is taking place as ''linear'' at all. This embracing awareness perceives, as the *Beowulf* poet sees in the passage quoted above, but as those in Heorot fortunately cannot, a larger pattern transcending the immediate experience. That is why such non-narrative visual analogies as ''interlace structure'' and my own art-term ''the baroque design of *Beowulf*'' (stressing the light-and-dark patterning in the poem) are valid as alternative descriptions, seeing the poem from a slightly different point-of-view than the linear structure of the narrative (the ''rising-falling'' or tripartite sequence).

That the poet himself built in this largest of effects, the invitation to a double view, I have no doubt, as he gives us hints at a number of points. Right at the beginning of the poem, for example, when Shield Shefing dies, his people set him adrift with many treasures in a beautiful ship, a death ship which in some sense is meant to carry his spirit to another world. Those in the world of the poem do not know, ''neither hall-councillors nor heroes under heaven / how to say what hands received that cargo'' (51–52). We know, however, because the poet has told us, that Shield Shefing is safe with God (37).

This static omniscient perspective is by no means a central feature of the poem, which is, after all, the narrative of a magnificent pagan hero, Beowulf, who fights three monsters in turn. But it is an embracing feature, and it should not be overlooked, for it explains much about the peculiarly patterned quality of the style.

Recommended Books

This list is selective and oriented toward the study of *Beowulf* in translation. Books on language and meter are not listed here, and books after 1984 are listed at the end.

Editions

Klaeber, Frederick, ed. *Beowulf and the Fight at Finnsburg*. 3rd ed. Boston: D. C. Heath, 1950.

Wrenn, C. L., ed. *Beowulf with the Finnesburg Fragment*. 2nd ed. London: Harrap, 1958. 3rd ed. Revised by W. F. Bolton. London: Harrap, 1973.

These are the two editions most useful for English-speaking students. The first is the most scholarly, and is referred to throughout both the notes and the Guide to Study. The second was prepared especially for students by the late Professor of Anglo-Saxon in the University of Oxford, C. L. Wrenn. It is more literary in approach and less heavy with notes and introduction; these have been updated recently by W. F. Bolton, but in my view the accessibility of the poem, which was Professor Wrenn's purpose in preparing his edition, has been diminished thereby. Bolton's introduction is interesting, however, for those who want an overview of recent scholarship (see also Chickering's translation cited below.)

Translations

Alexander, Michael. *Beowulf, a Verse Translation*. Harmondsworth: Penguin, 1973.

Chickering, Howell D., Jr. *Beowulf, a Dual-Language Edition*. New York: Anchor Books, 1977.

Clark Hall, J. R. *Beowulf and the Finnesburg Fragment, a Translation into Modern English Prose.* Revised by C. L. Wrenn. London: Allen and Unwin, 1961.

Crossley-Holland, Kevin. *Beowulf, a New Translation.* New York: Farrar, Straus and Giroux, 1968.

Donaldson, E. Talbot. *Beowulf: A New Prose Translation.* New York: W. W. Norton and Company, 1966.

Greenfield, Stanley A. *A Readable Beowulf.* Carbondale: Southern Illinois University Press, 1982.

Kennedy, Charles W. *Beowulf, the Oldest English Epic.* London: Oxford University Press, 1940.

Wright, David. *Beowulf: A Prose Translation.* Harmondsworth: Penguin, 1957.

These are the translations which seem to me best or most dependable, and I should like to comment briefly on their different qualities; I assume that you know about my own. Michael Alexander's translation gets precisely that density of language, or "grittiness," that I have decided to abandon for the sake of clarity. His avowed model is Ezra Pound. If one wants a more complicated, "modern" poem that is at the same time truer to the original in this one respect, Alexander's is the translation to read. Chickering's book is useful because of the facing page text and translation. His running commentary on major points of the poem is gracefully written and easy to digest, but his claim to have produced verse is one that I find hard to accept. Clark Hall was the classic when I was at Oxford, the prose translation that students depended upon before exams; Donaldson's, I believe, fills the same niche in American universities. Crossley-Holland's translation has many fine points, but now and again he takes a liberty with the text with which I do not agree. Greenfield's translation is based, curiously, on a syllabic verse-line, and in my view he goes astray in attempting to imitate the wordplay of the original, but it reads very well aloud. Kennedy's alliterative verse translation has been justly criticized for its "galloping" quality, and yet it was the version in which I first read the poem, and I found it fast and exciting. David Wright, like Michael Alexander and Kevin Crossley-Holland, is a known poet; he, however, has chosen to translate in prose. I find this by far the most graceful and stirring of the prose translations.

Record

A lively reading of passages from *Beowulf* (with translations provided) is that by J. B. Bessinger, *Beowulf, Caedmon's Hymn and Other Old English Poems* (Caedman Record Number T. C. 1161, 1962).

Anthologies of Articles

Fry, Donald K., ed. *The Beowulf Poet* (Twentieth Century Views). Englewood Cliffs, N.J.: Prentice-Hall, Inc., 1968.

Nicholson, Lewis E., ed. *An Anthology of Beowulf Criticism.* Notre Dame, Indiana: University of Notre Dame Press, 1963.

Tuso, Joseph F., ed. *Beowulf: The Donaldson Translation, Backgrounds and Sources, Criticism.* New York: W. W. Norton and Company, 1975.

Of these three paperback anthologies, I find Nicholson's the most useful, despite what has been criticized as the "pan-allegorical" tendency of a number of the contributors, who slant their reading of the poem toward a Christian interpretation. Two articles of major importance included in this anthology, not much concerned with the Christian/pagan argument, are C. L. Wrenn's "Sutton Hoo and *Beowulf*" and Francis P. Magoun, Jr.'s "The Oral Formulaic Character of Anglo-Saxon Narrative Poetry," All three anthologies include the one article that is absolutely essential outside reading for any serious student of the poem, J. R. R. Tolkien's British Academy Lecture, "*Beowulf,* the Monsters and the Critics."

A number of "festschrifts" honoring important scholars contain articles of special interest not yet otherwise anthologized, and others are to be found as chapters in books on more general subjects; many of these will be referred to in the notes and the guide. Single articles frequently appear in philological journals such as *Neuphilologische Mitteilungen, Studies in Philology,* and the *Journal of English and Germanic Philology,* more rarely in the more literary journals such as *PMLA* and specialist journals such as *Folklore.* A recently established annual devoted exclusively to studies in the field is *Anglo-Saxon England.*

Background Materials

Chambers, R. W. *Beowulf: An Introduction to the Study of the Poem.* 3rd ed., with supplement by C. L. Wrenn. London: Cambridge University Press, 1959.

Garmondsway, G. N., and Jacqueline Simpson, trans. *Beowulf and Its Analogues.* New York: E. P. Dutton, 1971.

Niles, John D. *Beowulf: The Poem and Its Tradition.* Cambridge, Mass.: Harvard University Press, 1983.

Whitelock, Dorothy. *The Audience of Beowulf.* Oxford: Oxford University Press, 1951.

Chamber's *Introduction* is the companion to the text that will be found in any serious scholar's library; it is a large volume of background material, both history and myth, with some tentative theorizing about date and structure. C. L. Wrenn's supplement is a survey of scholarship on *Beowulf* to 1959. Garmondsway and Simpson have brought together and translated (chiefly from Latin and Old Norse) all the important analogues to particular passages and digressions in the text; it is worth glancing through even if one is not prepared to do serious study in this area, simply to gain a sense of the broad literary and cultural tradition of which *Beowulf* is a part, quite alien to that which we with our cultural bias have named the ''great'' tradition. In her slim book, *The Audience of Beowulf,* Dorothy Whitelock is concerned in part with how the Germanic and Mediterranean traditions mesh in the poet's own Anglo-Saxon Christian culture, and how much he could expect his audience to know. Niles' book is the most recent wide-ranging study of the poem, published after my guide was written and addressing many matters from a fresh perspective. The various discussions are integrated by Niles' thesis that the poem is a post-Viking composition.

Literary Studies

Bonjour, Adrien. *The Digressions in Beowulf.* Oxford: Blackwell, 1950.

Brodeur, Arthur G. *The Art of Beowulf.* Berkeley: University of California Press, 1959.

Irving, Edward B., Jr. *A Reading of Beowulf.* New Haven and London: Yale University Press, 1968.

Sisam, Kenneth. *The Structure of Beowulf.* London: Oxford University Press, 1965.

J. R. R. Tolkien's lecture, "*Beowulf:* The Monsters and the Critics," reprinted in the Nicholson anthology cited above, is still, to my mind, the single most valuable work on *Beowulf* for any beginner in the literary study of the poem, and one to which those more experienced should frequently recur. By "putting the monsters back at the center," or viewing the main theme of the poem as of great symbolic interest transcending those historical matters with which scholars had been so absorbed in the past, Tolkien made literary appreciation of *Beowulf* respectable.

The books I cite here are those that I have found most useful concerning the literary style and structure of *Beowulf* exclusively. Bonjour's book, to which references will be found throughout the notes, is a careful evaluation of the way in which the various digression in the poem fit into their context and contribute to the unity of the poem as a whole. Brodeur's book is the first of its kind and discusses the major points of style and unity. Irving's more recent study is a lively literary commentary (abridged in his later *Introduction to Beowulf*) which students in particular should find illuminating. Sisam's book is negative criticism, a slim volume finding flaws in some of the main arguments scholars have proposed for the unity of the poem; I include it chiefly as a reminder that literary criticism is a exercise of the sympathetic imagination which needs a constant check in order to remain valid. (I review Bonjour, Brodeur and Sisam's ideas concerning structure in the section on that subject.)

Three recent books in which Anglo-Saxon poetry as a whole is discussed in innovative and illuminating ways are Stanley B. Greenfield's *A Critical History of Old English Literature* (New York: New York University Press, 1965), his *The Interpretation of Old English Poems* (London: Routledge and Kegan Paul, 1972), and T. A. Shippey's

Old English Verse (Hutchinson University Library, Atlantic Highlands, N.J.: Humanities Press, 1972). See also his recent slim volume *Beowulf* (Boston, Mass.: Charles River Books, 1979). Articles and books on particular points of style are cited in the chapter on style.

Bibliographies

Fry, Donald K. *Beowulf and the Fight at Finnsburg: A Bibliography*. Charlottesville: University of Virginia Press, 1969.

Robinson, Fred C. *Old English Literature: A Select Bibliography*. Toronto: University of Toronto Press, 1970. (Annotated.)

Robinson, Fred, and Greenfield, Stanley, eds. *A Complete Bibliography of Publications on Old English Literature from the Beginnings Through Nineteen Seventy-two*. Toronto: University of Toronto Press, 1980. (An exhaustive but very expensive bibliography, likely to be available only in major academic libraries.)

Short, Douglas D. *Beowulf Scholarship*. New York: Garland Press, 1980. (Extensive annotations of scholarship from 1950 to 1978.)

The Finnsburg Fragment and Episode

Fry, Donald K. *Finnsburg: Fragment and Episode*. London: Methuen, 1974. (Edition.)

Tolkien, J. R. R. *Finn and Hengest: The Fragment and the Episode*, edited by Alan Bliss. London: Allen and Unwin, 1982. (Edition and translation with textual notes and copious fascinating commentary.)

Date

Chase, Colin. *The Dating of Beowulf.* Toronto: University of Toronto Press, 1981. (The main arguments, including many for a ninth or tenth century date, are set out here.)

The book I would recommend for an understanding of the Anglo-Saxon period as a whole is *The Anglo-Saxons,* edited by James Campbell (Oxford: Phaidon, 1982). Heavily illustrated and containing articles by leading experts in various fields and periods of Anglo-Saxon history, it is essential reading for anyone wishing to understand the recent reevaluations of the date of *Beowulf.*

A Few Significant Books Published Since 1984

As before, these are selective and chosen with the new reader of *Beowulf* in mind.

Editions and Translations

Recent student editions of the poem have been published by George Jack (Oxford: Oxford University Press, 1994) and Bruce Mitchell and Fred C. Robinson (Oxford: Blackwell's, 1998). Klaeber's famously "standard" edition is currently being revised, with 2007 the estimated date of publication. The most exciting and innovative edition of the poem at this time, however, is Kevin Kiernan's *Electronic Beowulf*, of which there is a sample available online at http://www.uky.edu/~kiernan/eBeowulf/guide.htm.

The most notable recent translations are by Roy M. Liuzza, *Beowulf: A New Verse Translation* (Peterborough, Canada: Broadview Press, 2000), and by the Nobel Prize winner Seamus Heaney, *Beowulf: A New Verse Translation* (New York: Farrar, Straus and Giroux, 2000), with facing page original. This has also been republished without the original by W. W. Norton & Company, Inc. (New York, 2002). For information about these and other translations (and much else), see www.jagular.com/beowulf, a web page by the *Beowulf* "hobbyist," Syd Allan.

Anthologies

The two most useful recent anthologies in my opinion are *The Beowulf Reader*, edited by Peter S. Baker (New York: Garland, 1995), and *A Beowulf Handbook* (Lincoln: University of Nebraska Press, 1997), edited by Robert E. Bjork and John D. Niles and containing articles by specialists on most aspects of the poem. These anthologies supplement each other. Perhaps the best current anthology covering broader ground (not focused on *Beowulf*) is *Old English Literature: Critical Essays*, edited by R. M. Liuzza (New Haven: Yale University Press, 2002).

Background Materials

The most notable recent item here must be *Beowulf: The Critical Heritage*, edited by T. A. Shippey and Andreas Haarder (London: Routledge, 1998). George Clark's *Beowulf* (Boston: Twayne Publishers, 1990) is a good introductory study of the poem as a whole, and J. Michael Stitt's *Beowulf and the Bear's Son: Epic, Saga, and Fairytale in Northern Germanic Tradition* (New York: Garland, 1992) is a fascinating study of a particular aspect of the poem's background. At the time of this writing, John D. Niles is editing a book titled *Beowulf and Lejre*, reconsidering the physical location in Denmark in which the poet may have imagined Heorot (see p. 34 above).

Literary Studies

In *Beowulf and the Appositive Style* (Knoxville: University of Tennessee Press, 1985) Fred C. Robinson studies a range of language techniques to show how the poet achieves meanings and broadens them (including religious meaning); see also his essays in Part I of *The Tomb of Beowulf* (Oxford: Blackwell's, 1993). Gillian R. Overing was the first to bring postmodern critical theory to a study of the poem in *Language, Sign, and Gender in Beowulf* (Carbondale: Southern Illinois University Press, 1990). Overing's final chapter discusses gender issues.

Bibliography: Kevin Kiernan oversees an adapted bibliography of items published since 1990 at http://www.uky.edu/~kiernan/eBeowulf/beobib03.htm.